The Villein's Bible

The Villein's Bible

Stories in Romanesque Carving

Brian Young

BARRIE & JENKINS
LONDON

First published in Great Britain in 1990 by
Barrie & Jenkins Ltd
20 Vauxhall Bridge Road, London SW1V 2SA

British Library Cataloguing in Publication Data
Young, Brian
    The villein's Bible : stories in Romanesque carving.
    1. Europe. Churches. Gargoyles & grotesque carvings,
history
    I. Title
    729.5

ISBN 0-7126-3888-1

Designed by Peter Guy
Typeset by SX Composing, Rayleigh, Essex
Printed by Butler and Tanner Ltd, Frome

Contents

English and Spanish representations of this. The four creatures round Christ. Pentecost: exotic elements in the Vézelay tympanum. Several themes combined at Angoulême. The Last Judgment. Early use of Beatus' commentary, especially at Moissac. Later, Christ of the Passion is Judge, and the parable of the Sheep and Goats is used. Conques: a less spiritual Judgment. Autun: saved and damned equally finely represented. The impact of visions on spectators: Malmesbury. The kindling of devotion is the aim of all religious art: Romanesque carving achieves this with poignant simplicity, and has much to offer our age.

Introduction

'In the Middle Ages men had no great thought
that they did not write down in stone.'
                                            VICTOR HUGO

I ONCE KNEW A MAN who did not greatly care for Romanesque carving, even when the best of it was put before him;
and his gratitude afterwards was delightfully ambiguous –
'We do thank you for telling us so much that was new:
we've been boring our friends with it ever since'. But he was
surely the exception. To many people the portrayal of
scenes and figures from the period roughly between 1000
and 1250 A.D., usually the work of anonymous carvers, is
as exciting and interesting as any artistic experience. There
is great dignity, as well as simplicity, in the depiction; the
style is direct and energetic, with figures that are now majestic, now animated; the tone is highly expressive; the
gestures and looks convey strong emotion – but generally
with restraint; and there is a powerful sense of the spiritual
quality of man which makes the work somehow nobler than
the most accurate representation (whether from Classical or
from later times) of how people in fact appear when propor-
tion and perspective are mastered. There can be no doubt
then that the beauties of the Romanesque style can move the
viewer profoundly, even though the damage inflicted by
time or by man, and the difficulty of getting close enough to
the carving, may sometimes lead to disappointment.

Why then, in an age rich in books and television pro-
grammes, are our chances of admiring and enjoying this
work so limited? In the first place, old carvings are less
accessible than paintings: a wealth of pictures is con-
veniently gathered in many a gallery and big house, so that
the greatness of El Greco or Rembrandt or Turner forces
itself on the attention of any lover of art. Moreover, there
are only a few countries which possess the treasures of
Romanesque carving; and England, though it has more
than some suppose, is far behind France and Italy and
Northern Spain in the riches of its early medieval sculpture.
Almost every work either strikes the eye at random, unaided
by a convenient label or explanation, or else requires a

special journey; many of the churches which contain the finest carvings are in fairly remote parts, where there was less later wealth to encourage fashionable rebuilding or disastrous restoration. While English museums, such as those in London and York, offer some attractive bits and pieces, these are only fragmentary; and one special feature of Romanesque sculpture is that it is best seen in place, closely related to the architecture and atmosphere of the church to which it belongs. One more obstacle to appreciating this glorious tradition is the problem of reading its message, of seeing (often beneath decay and damage) what the artist was trying to do, and of entering the hearts and minds of those to whom this art first spoke.

All these difficulties, which can interfere with appreciation of Romanesque carving, point to the need for good reproduction of the scenes that are represented – and for a text which combines enjoyment of the sculpture with a closer understanding of the Bible. So my purpose has been to gather together some of the finest examples of Romanesque narrative carving, to discuss the reasons for their often strange appearance, and to place them firmly in their Biblical setting. For they were, for centuries, the picture Bible of those who could not read – telling the stories, drawing the lessons, encouraging steadfastness in bad times, and warning of judgment to come. The early medieval approach to the Bible may seem naïve, so that the trumpet gives an uncertain sound to modern believers. Something is said here, therefore, about the Christian meanings and ideas which obtained in medieval times – as well as about the artistic origins and conventions of the style. As the background (in word and art) is better understood, the message for today grows more valid, and begins to have the significance which the people of those days prized.

The full range of carvings touches an interest not only in art history and theology but also in medieval life. However, the secular carvings of everyday activities and the labours of the months (not to mention the random creatures and monsters and plants) are for the most part beyond the scope of this book. For in the main it was the Bible that fascinated the greatest medieval carvers; and to cover even that fully would require more room than is here available.

This text, with matching illustrations, is therefore an introduction to the Bible as it appears in Romanesque carvings. No such introduction exists; and I hope this book will appeal to lovers of art and to lovers of the Bible, and also to travellers who may be – or become – one or both of these. The reader who then wants more original research and scholarship must seek out those whose honey I have sipped, the art historians, iconographers, theologians, and medievalists, whose studies are more esoteric.

My reason for providing the introduction is that, when sightseeing, I found myself increasingly drawn to the style in which early medieval carvers presented scenes from the Bible. In addition, the dramatic qualities of such carving made it the sculptural equivalent of opera; and deciding whom the figures in an obscure carving might represent had a strong appeal as problem-solving. Photographs which I took on my travels became less concerned with people and landscape and more with the carved detail of Romanesque churches. I directed my steps, both in Britain and overseas, to places where early medieval sculpture could be seen; and invitations from Serenissima Travel to accompany tours as a guest-lecturer made possible further travel in France, Italy, Spain and Eastern Turkey.

It was natural to read what art historians had to say about the Romanesque style, and this too I found intriguing. Earlier, my study of the Bible had been stimulated by having to teach and preach, as well as by church services: this interacted with my enjoyment of the carving, as I hope it will for the reader. In this book Bible references are given, for those who wish to recall a story more fully; quotations in the text are usually from my memory of the Authorized Version, unless that translation seems faulty or obscure.

'Romanesque' (often referred to in Britain as 'Norman') is a late term, and learned ink is spilt over the question of when it begins and ends. Yet, with all the differences of style and period and area of origin, there is a family likeness about the work. This likeness has led me to include some Armenian sculpture of a period before 1000 A.D., while omitting Anglo-Saxon work and most Ottonian gold and ivory carvings. It has also led me to exclude, at the end of the period, the marvellous sculpture of Chartres and Bourges, and the Italian work of the great Pisano family; for these seem nearer in spirit to the Gothic. Not everyone will agree about these exclusions; but in drawing lines personal taste can help guide the pen. The sculpture of Romanesque tympana and capitals and fonts and lintels, the panels of bronze doors, and the early wooden crucifixes are riches enough: they make a powerful lens for seeing the bible that was read and preached to unlettered medieval man – the 'villein' of my title.

BRIAN YOUNG

The Villein's Bible

1. Old Testament

THE FIRST PAGES of the Bible mattered more to the medieval carver than any other part of the Old Testament; for here was the second of the two Creation accounts, the Adam and Eve story[a]. This told the tale of how sin first came into the world in a splendidly pictorial way. It is fitting that the simple but profound quality of this story should be matched by the style of a great Lombard sculptor, Wiligelmo. He worked in Modena, around 1100, and there various influences came together: the ruins of Roman classical art, especially on sarcophagi, suggested a frieze in bas-relief, with no very close relationship to the surrounding architecture; the links between North Italy and Germany gave contact with metal-workers to the north, who had developed a tone of dignified severity, with touches both human and spiritual; and a desire to tell stories simply to those who could not read made for a vivid directness of style.

So, in Modena cathedral, a grave God is seen creating Adam, and then drawing Eve from his side while he sleeps. Further on in the series of events, the Fall of Man takes place; and a gleeful serpent looks across as Adam eats the apple and shame begins to dawn on him and his wife. We see movement and diagonal lines now, whereas the art of Byzantium had been static and vertical; but it is a heavy movement, unlike the dancing mannerism of some French carvers of the period – even though it is possible that Wiligelmo, who may himself have been a German, was familiar with the work of contemporary Frenchmen. The general effect is massive and homely; but it has the power to move the viewer thanks to its intensity and simple gestures.

It is immediately apparent from this work that Romanesque sculpture does not return to the round form of the free-standing statue. For centuries now, the relief has been the usual style of carving: it is intended to be seen from the front alone, and it is nearly flat in its adornment of a surface. Nevertheless, it creates a three-dimensional impression, of a kind that is not yet possible for painters. The nearest approach in this period to the marble sculpture of earlier times, able to be viewed from various angles, is perhaps the

1 *left* Modena. Cathedral. Creation of Adam and Eve
2 *above* Modena. Cathedral. The Fall

Archbishop's throne at Bari: this may itself be the work of Wiligelmo, though there is no agreement on this. Two prisoners, who are not part of any Biblical narrative, hold up this throne; they are almost in the round, and the fluidity of their exertions gives a most striking impression of the skill which sculptors already had at their command.

Even more elementary than the Modena reliefs, though still suffused with stocky vigour, is their nearest English equivalent, that which decorates a font at East Meon in Hampshire. The creation of Adam and Eve has the naïve 3 look which reminds us of the Modena portrayal of the same scenes; and it is followed by an encounter between Eve and 4 a most lively serpent. This work is particularly dependent

3 *above* East Meon. Church. Creation of Adam and Eve
4 *below* East Meon. Church. Adam, Eve and the serpent
5 *opposite* Santiago. Cathedral. God and Adam

on the metalwork of Northern Europe; for the font is in fact Flemish, from Tournai. The Carolingian and Ottonian craftsmen of the ninth and tenth centuries laid a foundation for the stone-carving of the Romanesque period: in the words of Peter Lasko, 'In the transforming of even the most fluid of styles towards a firm pictorial structure, and in the domination of the picture space by the human figure in the service of expressive narrative, the first [Ottonian] steps towards Romanesque were taken'. The stark quality and blackness of the East Meon font recall another font nearby in Winchester cathedral which, though it does not address itself to the Bible story, is also Flemish and owes much to earlier metal-workers.

It is easy to see why the story of Adam and Eve should be the most popular of all Old Testament narratives. It accounts for a central human weakness by portraying the Fall of Man. The continuing significance of this lies not in the tree and the fruit (which is nowhere said to be an apple – but 'apple' and 'evil' are the same word in Latin, and this had its effect). Nor is the story about sexuality. Its real significance lies in the fact that man, as his awareness increases, makes himself, rather than God, the centre of his world ('Ye shall be as gods'). The story of the Redemption tells of Christ reversing this propensity of man to make self the centre: for he 'did not count equality with God a thing to be grasped' [b] – an echo surely of the taking of the fruit by Adam and Eve. The Fall, a profound myth about human sinfulness, and the Redemption, which restores love as triumphant over self-concern, were rightly central doctrines for the medieval Christian.

It is not always the case that the primitive setting of the story is reflected in primitive sculpture. A carving at Santiago of God commissioning Adam at the creation of the world shows considerable sophistication, and the slimness and suavity of the figures makes a contrast with the heavy breadth of those at Modena. Even more strikingly, the Eve at Autun, which formerly lay along a lintel of the cathedral, is one of the most sensuous of all Romanesque sculptures. Here Eve whispers to Adam and guiltily plucks the fruit without looking at it; a devilish hand can just be seen bending the tree towards her. Wickedness has indeed come into the world; and Gislebertus, the Autun sculptor, is well in advance of his time in the way he portrays it.

Very different in mood is a capital at Clermont-Ferrand which shows the expulsion from the garden: there the avenging angel grasps Adam by the beard, while Adam not only seizes Eve by the hair but also kicks her. In other carvings of the expulsion God's attitude is shown in very human style. At Hildesheim he is severe in his accusation, and the blame is duly passed on in a bare but vivid cameo. It is worth noticing here that the trees seem to echo the stance of Adam and Eve. A milder spirit is apparent in a carving at Cluny, which may possibly be the work of the same Gislebertus, before he moved to Autun: here God is sad with reproach, as he raises his hands in sorrow at man's misuse of his free-will. A similar gesture can be seen, with three marvellous faces, on the portal of the church of Santa Maria at Uncastillo.

Cluny, in southern Burgundy, which was largely demolished after being wrecked in the anti-clerical fervour of the French Revolution, was the greatest of abbeys in the eleventh century, answerable directly to the Pope. It had a

6 *above* Autun. Museum. Eve
7 *opposite, above* Hildesheim. Cathedral door. God, Adam, and Eve
8 *opposite, left* Cluny. Museum. God, Adam, and Eve
9 *opposite, right* Uncastillo. Santa Maria Church. God, Adam, and Eve

profound influence on figurative carving, since the Bene-
dictines there gave strong encouragement to representative
images of the faith (as against the avoidance of these by
Muslims and other non-Christian people). Sculptors of rare
genius adorned the abbeys and churches of many dependencies of Cluny. Romanesque sculpture can best be seen
therefore in Burgundy, in Languedoc, and all along the
roads leading south-west to Santiago de Compostela. Cluniac influence spread along these, both for holy pilgrimage
and for a holy crusade against the Muslims in Spain which
preceded the first crusade to the Holy Land by thirty years
or so. Uncastillo is a little-known but impressive example of
a town affected by the pilgrim routes to Santiago.

The Cluniac influence began soon after 1000 A.D. From
that year, as it became apparent that the millennium had not
brought about the Second Coming, the earth flowered with
new churches. Many abbeys which were daughter-houses
of Cluny drew together the themes which had come from
Byzantium and the styles which ivories, metalwork and
manuscripts had made familiar: these were combined with
the liturgy and teaching of the church and with fresh theo-
logical insights to furnish material for the new talents of
stone-carvers.

The first half of the twelfth century was the great age of
Romanesque sculpture, and the inspiration of Cluny made
it so. But the style did not hold the field for very long. By the
middle of the century, Northern France was drawing on the
genius of the southern carvers, and, under Abbot Suger of
St. Denis, soon moved on to Gothic sculpture with its
greater concern for idealized physical beauty. Meanwhile
the Cistercians, influenced by their founder, St. Bernard of
Clairvaux, who despised the Cluniac representation of
animals and people, sought beauty in the simplicity of architecture, and rejected narrative sculpture. Many famous
ruined abbeys in Britain are Cistercian in origin; so there is
disappointment for those who look on their battered walls
for the stone bibles that are such a glory in France.

The themes of narrative sculpture naturally followed the
understanding men had of the Bible. The Old Testament
was the beginning of a long story of Redemption that
reached its climax in the New Testament: even Adam's sin
was a fortunate event, according to St. Augustine, since it
won so great a redeemer. Medieval man looked back at the

early books of the Bible with eyes that had read the later books, and valued Old Testament stories principally as these found fulfilment in Christianity. (A rather similar interpretation of the pagan stories of Greece and Rome arose in early Renaissance times: these first gained acceptance because they were held to be heathen strivings after God's truth). Stories from the Old Testament usually appear in Romanesque carving, therefore, because they are 'types', prefiguring something from the later story of man's redemption. This is true even of details in the Creation story, though the account of man's fall is the central issue. For example, more is often made of the creation of Eve than of the creation of Adam. This is not through regard for women, nor just because it is more graphic: it is because Eve rising from Adam's rib was a 'type' of the church springing up from Christ's wounded side. A simpler foreshadowing can be seen in an image of Eve on the doors of Hildesheim cathedral: here Eve, suckling her babe after the Fall, points forward to the Virgin Mary, the second Eve, as her posture calls to mind representations of the Madonna. These Hildesheim doors are Ottonian and of very early date (just after 1000 A.D.); yet the style of the reliefs has moved far beyond the childish roughness which often characterizes

10 Hildesheim. Cathedral door. Eve suckling Cain

primitive work. Already there is the strength of gesture and emotion, and the powerful simplicity and directness, which later make the best Romanesque work so appealing.

Since the Old Testament foreshadows the New, at Hildesheim the story of the Fall is balanced by the story of the Redemption – a correspondence of scenes which becomes much more common and more detailed from the middle of the twelfth century onwards. The thought of Christ, the second Adam, coming to earth to undo man's original wrong led naturally to the inclusion, in carvings of Christ's life, of scenes of the Fall. At Pisa, on another fine door, the Wise Men bring the nations back to God, while underneath them the rejection of God in Genesis is portrayed. Christ's cross sometimes, as on a crucifix in the Federic Marés Museum at Barcelona, has a small figure of Adam at its foot. This was because a picturesque early legend had Adam's sin annulled by imagining Golgotha as the place of his burial, and treating the cross as the tree from Eden, dead for many centuries but breaking into bloom again when the Fall of Man was reversed by Christ.

Another legend, based on a sentence in the first epistle of Peter[c], told of Christ's descent into hell to save the souls of those just persons who lived before his time; and the main feature of this was the 'Anastasis', or raising of Adam who (in the words of the carol) 'lay y-bounden'. On the font at Eardisley there is splendid energy in the naïve but attractive carving of this scene. Man is redeemed as Adam is hauled up out of the tangles of sin. Such tangles well suit the Herefordshire school of carving, since these carvers loved to fill all the

11 *opposite* Pisa. Cathedral door.
  Magi, with Fall of Man
12 *above* Barcelona. F. Marés Museum.
  Crucifix, with Adam
13 *right* Eardisley. Church font.
  Christ saves Adam

space with decoration. This tendency derived from Northern influences, and is visible in Norwegian churches; the tradition of Vikings and Celts, like some Eastern traditions, had less care for the representation of people than for the elaboration of ornament. The Herefordshire carvers also liked to portray birds: hence the appearance of the Holy Spirit here, following a hint in the passage quoted from St. Peter's first epistle.

The southern, classical tradition is quite different. The very word 'Romanesque' implies a connection between medieval carving and the old style of sculpture which the Romans had practised. In fact, the word was coined in the nineteenth century, both because Romanesque arches were round like Roman ones, and to suggest that 'Romanesque' had sprung from 'Roman' much as the Romance languages had sprung from the Latin language. It was a description which, like the words 'Gothic' and 'Baroque', was intended to disparage the style it so named; it pictured Romanesque as a debased form which did not equal the realistic effects of Classicism. A high regard for realism, and a respect for Classical perfection, lasted for many centuries, and contributed to the feeling that Romanesque was inferior and that its carvings were rude or quaint; it was only in the late nineteenth and early twentieth centuries, when artists were exploring other ways than realism of expressing truth, that the Romanesque style came to be properly valued, and its remains rightly treasured. But to imply that Romanesque means an inferior version of Roman is in any case mistaken: except in Provence, and in one or two other localities, the Roman influence, representing human beings accurately but with less sense of their inner life, had limited effect on Romanesque work. Indeed, the style owes quite as much to the East and the North as it does to Rome.

In Genesis, and in the carvings, Adam's primal selfishness leads to more overt crime. First, Cain and Abel make their different offerings[d]. At St. Gilles du Gard we see a grave but graceful movement, probably copied from a Byzantine model. This flows more sweetly than is usual in the sculpture of Provence, where, as I have just mentioned, Roman influences generally continued to shape carving in a classical style. God (here, as often, represented by a pointing hand) shows favour to Abel's animal offering. The reason why this should be so does not matter – though one of the story's

14 St. Gilles du Gard. Abbey church. Cain and Abel make their offerings

attractions for the medieval clergy was a warning it was held to contain against the niggardly payment of tithes. The real lesson is that anger now, in a fallen world, leads on to violence, as Cain kills Abel. This scene is well shown at Monreale on yet another set of bronze doors. In the sequence of events on the Hildesheim doors too the killing of Abel is unforgettable. After the murder (and to the left of the Hildesheim panel) come the judgment and punishing of Cain. A capital at Autun shows God questioning him – 'Where is Abel thy brother?' Different interpretations have been placed on this carving, but it is now clear, from the body of Abel in the bushes, that the two figures seen must be God and Cain; the expression of guilt on the face of Cain is very fine.

Later, murder becomes more sophisticated, as weapons

are invented. 'Who could possibly kill Cain?' was once a question for the sceptic, when the Genesis story was taken as literal truth rather than as one of the profoundest of stories about man's condition. The answer of the rabbis and of later myth – though not of Genesis – was that the deed was done by Cain's great-great-great-grandson, Lamech, who certainly boasted of killing many men[e]. In the Modena sequence, a powerful arrow-shot from Lamech (a figure with a certain Assyrian quality) pierces Cain to the heart. A close look at Lamech's face indicates that he is blind; for, in some versions of the story, he lost his sight in his old age and mistook Cain for a wild beast in the thicket. There is also a further refinement of the tale which said that the hand of Lamech was guided by his son, Tubal-Cain, who was the legendary inventor of bronze and iron. This version is

powerfully portrayed on another of the capitals at Autun.

The later characters in Genesis are much less commonly seen in carvings than Adam and Eve. But several of them not only have a story from which the carver can fashion a capital or tympanum but also have significance as prefiguring either New Testament events or the later history of the church. The story of Noah [f], for example, appears quite often for a good symbolic reason: the ark which delivers a chosen few from the flood prefigures the church saving believers from the perils and wickedness of the world. At Monreale we see a most dignified picture of two animals being welcomed into the ark by Noah. Less edifying is the tale that follows in the Bible story, of Noah's drunkenness; when, very occasionally, this is shown, the reason is that Ham's behaviour was held to be a 'type' of the mocking of Christ.

Much more obvious in its lesson, since it foreshadows the Crucifixion, is Abraham's readiness to sacrifice his son [g]. A noble portrayal of this scene appears at Akhtamar, an island in Lake Van famous for its one building, the church of the Holy Cross. The stone carvings at Akhtamar are perhaps the earliest that seem Romanesque in style; they date from the early tenth century and belong to an Armenian tradition which, though distant, may well have had an influence on Western European work. The evidence is not conclusive; but a recent book (*Origins of the Romanesque* by V. I. Atroschenko and Judith Collins) makes a strong case for a link between Armenian sculpture and the Romanesque sculpture of a century or two later. In this particular scene the gravity of Abraham, as his eyes turn towards the angel of the Lord, makes a fine counterpoint with the innocent simplicity of Isaac and the ram. In Barcelona there is an equally impressive carving of the event. Here, by contrast, we see strong emotion in all the characters (including the ram, who in this interpretation well knows what is coming to him). Isaac's carrying of the wood is sometimes shown also: this prefigures the carrying of the cross by Christ.

Though Genesis is a prime source of stories seen in carvings, there are plenty of good pictures for sculptors in other Old Testament books. We have seen two ways in which an Old Testament character qualifies for an appearance in early medieval carving: the first is that his story has a pictorial interest, so that he can be identified in the sculpture

19 *opposite, top left* Autun. Cathedral. Lamech kills Cain
20 *opposite, top right* Monreale. Cathedral door. Noah
21 *above* Akhtamar. Church. Abraham and Isaac
22 *opposite, below* Barcelona. Museum of Catalan art. Abraham and Isaac

through the event in which he plays a part; the second, which is quite as important, is that in some way he points forward. I have written of 'types', of 'prefiguring', of 'foreshadowing': all these words are used of the same essential quality – that the character in the Old Testament prophesies, or finds fulfilment in, the infinitely more important story of Christ which is contained in the New Testament.

So key figures in the Old Testament are those with whom Christ compares himself: he tells us that 'a greater than Solomon is here',[h] and we may expect therefore to find some representations of that king. The most pictorial event in Solomon's life is the wise judgment in which he allots a disputed child to the woman who chooses to see the child given to another woman rather than see it killed[i]. This scene can be studied at Najera on the sarcophagus of Doña Blanca of Navarre; its appearance near to a carving of the Wise Men might suggest that it represents the Massacre of the Innocents, since a man with a raised sword is holding an infant upside down in his other hand. But the presence on one side of a woman kneeling for a blessing from a kingly figure, and on the other side of a woman impassively watching the threatened killing, make it plain that this is in fact the Judgment of Solomon.

An even more powerful depiction of this scene appears on a Westminster Abbey capital, which is now to be seen in the cloister museum. The face of the kneeling woman here reminds me of the Chichester carvings more than of contemporary French or Spanish work; it may not be too fanciful to see some link between these sculptures.

It is fitting that a royal abbey should commemorate royal wisdom. But this Solomon capital, now only a fragment displaced from its original position, is one of the few Romanesque carvings to be found in large cities. In such places cathedrals and churches rarely show survivals from this early period. In the heart of wealth and constant rebuilding, the early medieval style was too easily despised as simple in the following centuries; and in the centre of action great carving was too often shattered later on by intolerance of one kind or another.

Jonah is another example of prefiguring used by Christ himself in the same passage[j], since his three days in the whale's belly are a 'type' of Christ's three days in the tomb, and since he was a sign to the people of Nineveh as Christ

24 *above* Westminster. Abbey. Judgment of Solomon

23 *above* Najera. Abbey church. Judgment of Solomon

was a sign to the men of his age. The story of Jonah appears on the church at Akhtamar, in a kind of strip, with oriental overtones. For facial expression, however, I prefer the encounter between David and Goliath[k] at Akhtamar; one notices here the sly confidence of David, the power (with a hint of concern) of the huge Goliath in his Byzantine armour and the uncertainty of the least important (and therefore smallest) figure on the scene, the robed King Saul.

David's position as a forerunner, indeed an ancestor, of Christ is also referred to in the New Testament. The linking of the two can be seen in a carving of the Crucifixion which appears later. But his triumph over the mighty Philistine, Goliath, is intended to encourage the anxious believer to

25 *above* Akhtamar. Church. David and Goliath
26 *opposite, top left* St. Aignan. Church. Daniel and the lions
27 *opposite, top right* Worms. Cathedral. Daniel and the lions
28 *opposite, below* Stretton Sugwas. Church. Samson and the lion

trust in deliverance. The same is true of Daniel; he had long been a popular subject of carvings, for here there was scope for the artist to portray lions, which would have been familiar to him from many illustrations, as well as to depict a human being. At St. Aignan, in a small church on the Cher, Daniel has good cause for his anxious prayer, since the lions are full of gleeful menace[l]. But it is not unusual to see the lions gambolling on each side of Daniel, to illustrate the conclusion of the story when they are tamed and do not harm him. At Worms the German carver strikes an even softer note, with the lions showing affection for the prophet.

Lions have various symbolic meanings in Romanesque carving when they are anything more than mere decoration: sometimes they are good, partly because of the strange belief that they licked their dead cubs to revive them, so prefiguring the Resurrection; but often they are bad, standing for the forces of evil. ('Deliver them from the mouth of the lion', says the ancient prayer). When a lion fights against Samson[m], as at Stretton Sugwas, it is of course on the wrong side. This representation is pretty basic. The lion fills the tympanum (the semi-circular space between flat lintel and round arch) very agreeably. But, apart from the calm determination of Samson, there is less spirit here than in the best

29 *above* Moissac. Abbey cloister. Samson and the lion
30 *right* Avignon. (now in Fogg Museum, Cambridge, Mass.). Samson pulls down the temple

[34]

of the Herefordshire carvings. Some of the Herefordshire inspiration, especially at Kilpeck, apparently derives from a carver's visit to south-west France; and, if we look at one depiction of Samson and the lion, from Moissac, we see beneath the damage a deeper and more forceful effect, the result of the much more accomplished technique of those who worked on the pilgrim routes.

More dramatic still is Samson's action in pulling down the columns of the Philistines' temple[n]. The most striking representation of this was originally in a cloister at Avignon and is now in the Fogg Museum in the United States. The faces of the Philistines which appear in the openings of the temple above Samson add a delightful but naïve touch; similar shocked worshippers can be seen in the capital at Autun depicting the same scene – but there the anxiety is worse since the pillar of the temple has already been moved. Samson's various triumphs over evil make a dramatic story, with several opportunities for the carver. At Akhtamar there is a figure who must be Samson. It may be surprising that his face has a certain sweetness; but he is nevertheless

on the point of killing (though his victim here is a Philistine rather than a lion), and the object in his right hand is surely the jawbone of an ass[o].

A live ass looks soulfully out from a capital at Saulieu. It is standing fast, obedient to the word of God. Its rider, Balaam, does not see the angel[p] but is rebuked by his ass. Why should so unimportant a character, who was later killed with the idolatrous Midianites, be worth recording on a capital? The answer lies in his prophecies later, where one line[q] was thought to predict the star of the Nativity – a star seen by the Magi who, like Balaam, were Gentiles. But, in case that is not enough, he is also a type of someone in the New Testament: it is Doubting Thomas.

Balaam was a prophet with a simple pictorial story. But the later prophets, though they are far more important in the Bible story, offer few scenes for the carver; and the same is true of intensely poetic books like the Psalms and the discussions in Job. Elijah, however, driving his chariot up to heaven[r], clearly earns his place, as a forerunner of Christ ascending to God. Again, the animals help to make a good

31 *above* Akhtamar. Church. Samson
32 *left* Saulieu. Abbey church. Balaam

picture, whether the style, as at Fidenza, is grim and archaic, 3
with echoes of Wiligelmo, or more fluid and animated, as on
the magnificent bronze doors which are now in Novgorod. 3
These doors have a strange history. They are in no sense
Russian, for they were certainly cast in Germany. Their des-
tination was a cathedral which was Polish. To add to the
cosmopolitan story, some have maintained that the makers
of these doors were Italian; it is also suggested that the nearest stylistic likeness to them is in Spain, on the badly-
damaged but majestic portal at Ripoll. All this underlines
the fact that Romanesque art was anything but parochial.

Moses is, of course, primarily a lawgiver, as well as an important leader of the Israelites. His main significance lies in
the fact that he brought down the Ten Commandments
from Sinai. For this reason, it is he who represents the law,
whereas Elijah represents the prophets, in carvings of the
Transfiguration. The two stand on either side of Christ, as 1
symbolic forerunners of one who fulfilled both the law and
the prophets. Moses' crossing of the Red Sea[s] is also sometimes shown on fonts, as at Hildesheim, to prefigure 3
Christ's baptism. When he stands alone, Moses can at times
be recognized by the tablets of the law, or, as at Augsburg, 3
by the serpent which he lifts up – another prefiguring mentioned by Christ himself[t]. In later sculpture he is identifiable
by a very curious feature: he has a pair of horns on his
head, as in Michelangelo's famous statue. This is entirely
due to a mistranslation: when he came down from Sinai

33 *opposite, top right* Fidenza. Cathedral. Elijah
34 *opposite, top left* Novgorod. Cathedral door. Elijah
35 *above* Hildesheim. Cathedral font. Moses crosses the Red Sea
36 *opposite, below* Augsburg. Cathedral door. Moses and the serpent

37 *opposite* Moissac.
   Abbey church.
   Prophet
   (perhaps Jeremiah)
38 *right* Souillac.
   Abbey church. Isaiah

[38]

'with the skin of his face shining'[u], this was rendered as 'cornutus' (horned) by Jerome, in his Vulgate translation of the Bible.

Patriarchs and prophets from the Old Testament appear so often as single figures that one cannot show a full selection. In the following age, when Gothic buildings gave more height and light, the single figure, standing in niche or portal, became more common than the sort of scene that fitted the Romanesque tympanum or capital. Within the period which concerns us, however, it is worth looking at three particular single figures from the Old Testament: these have been chosen deliberately to counter the impression that the Romanesque style is static, stiff, and ponderous. However great the dignity and gravity that mark many early medieval carvings, it is worth stressing that fluidity and movement can also be seen, even in a single character who stands alone and is not part of a scene of action.

The figure of a prophet (who has often been identified as Jeremiah) stands in the pillar, or trumeau, at Moissac, supporting the vast lintel and tympanum of this most impressive portal. In ancient times, and in much Lombard sculpture, such a figure would have been an atlas, or telamon (or, if female, a caryatid), with a size and posture that probably gave some indication of the weight being carried. But here the reverse is true: almost dancing, with a grave but ecstatic step, the prophet seems to soar effortlessly away from bearing the load. The exaggerated twist of the body and the tilt of the head bring to mind the style to which later ages gave the name of Mannerism. So this long flowing figure has a restless energy and a refined elegance which give him an extraordinary grace amid his solid surroundings.

Another prophet, the Isaiah at Souillac, is even more substantial and lifelike; yet he too is carved with an exquisite rapture of movement. His body and arms and legs are all flexed so that they touch the surrounding frame at many points; this produces a series of triangles around his sinuous form. It has been convincingly argued, by Henri Focillon, that this image of movement is not just a whim of the sculptor: geometrical rules demand that the picture fills the frame, in accordance with a decorative instinct which, from early ornamental traditions, hates a vacuum. The result is that figures often seem to be dancing, or climbing, or (like the Eve at Autun) swimming. Another possible source of the

39 Santiago.
Cathedral. David

length and vivacity of these figures is the work of illuminators: their calligraphy affected the illustration of their manuscripts, and the illuminated manuscripts in their turn had a widespread effect on carving. This influence can be seen in other Romanesque details too – the clothes clinging to the body, the concentric folds on chest and knees, and the flaring drapery. Whatever may have been the origins of the style, the impression of movement and sway in much early medieval sculpture is imaginative and fluent; there is a tension between the static and the dynamic which is a major Romanesque accomplishment.

Even a seated figure can give this impression of movement: the crossed legs and nonchalant air of King David at Santiago, with a pose perhaps copied from a carving still to be seen at Toulouse, suggest one who is musician as well as hero. The sculpture provides another example of the lightness and grace of many carvers who worked at the beginning of the twelfth century and who transformed the solid immobility which marked the very first sculptures seen along the Pilgrim Route.

Already, having looked only at scenes and figures taken from the Old Testament, we can see how widespread are the examples of Romanesque carving: they reach from Herefordshire and Santiago in the west to Armenian Akhtamar, now in Turkey, in the east, and from Novgorod in northern Russia to Monreale in Sicily.

Yet the Old Testament, important as it was to medieval man, only helped the Christian look forward to the story of Jesus, who both redeemed its loss and fulfilled its highest hopes. To his life we now turn.

2. Nativity

THE COMING OF CHRIST to earth at Christmas is a central element in the Christian faith; and so the Incarnation, in which Our Lord takes on human flesh, is a mystery that artists, as well as thinkers, address with their best gifts. Yet, as every Christian recalls, the story of Christ's birth is told by two writers only – Matthew[a] and Luke[b]. It has been said that Matthew's account derives from Joseph's memory of the first Christmas, and Luke's account from Mary's; these are indeed the only two possible sources if what we read is history in human terms. A plainer difference between the two is that Matthew writes for the Jews, and constantly stresses the fulfilment of prophecy: paradoxically this means that he tells the story of the Magi, which is often taken as a symbol of the world outside Israel coming to Christ. Luke writes primarily for the Gentile world, though his account of the Nativity is deeply influenced by Old Testament writing: his concern for the universality of the gospel is reflected in his narration of the visit of the shepherds to the manger – Jews indeed, but poor and simple folk. These two accounts are regularly combined by the carvers, who show shepherds and wise men coming to the manger at the same time. Later on, the two stories are more difficult to harmonize in a single narrative: Matthew describes a flight into Egypt, seeing the return from there as fulfilling history and prophecy from the Old Testament; Luke writes of the presentation of Christ in the temple, followed immediately by a return to Nazareth. But sculpture still has no problem in combining events from both accounts.

The Annunciation heralds the story of Christ's birth. To indicate that someone is speaking, sculptor and painter normally showed a raised right hand with one or two fingers pointing upwards. The angel of the Annunciation at Moissac is an example of this helpful convention, though the face here must be a restoration since it has a soft sweetness which is not typical of the Romanesque. Another convention for speech is to have the character holding a scroll, on which his words are written out. This is more helpful still, though it makes for artificiality, rather like the frames

40 Moissac. Abbey church. Annunciation

41 *right* Conques. Abbey church. Annunciation
42 *opposite* Monreale. Cathedral cloister. Annunciation

of script in old silent films. A beautiful Annunciation on a capital at Conques shows the angel, whose name is Gabriel, carrying his story on a scroll. Much of the carving at Conques is rather stiff and formal, and seems to be more closely related to work from Auvergne, to the north-east, than to work from Languedoc, to the south-west. But this Annunciation has some of the intensity and depth of the Languedoc sculptures, and bears comparison with the more famous sequence from Moissac.

There are further conventions for carvings of the Annunciation. Gabriel usually walks in rather than flies down. Mary expresses her astonishment, awe, and acceptance by raising her hands with palms facing outwards; sometimes, as at Conques, she raises one hand only since the other grasps the symbol of the work she has been doing, a spindle.

An Eastern legend held that she was spinning thread for the veil of the Temple at Jerusalem (the same veil that was 'rent in twain' at the Crucifixion).

The suggestion of Mary's work with a spindle being interrupted can also be seen in a carving from the cloisters at Monreale. When the architecture offers a double frame, as here, the figures of Mary and Gabriel are widely separated. But the confines of one small capital, such as that in Gerona, often bring the two closely together; this fairly represents

43 *above* Villafranca del Bierzo.
St. James church.
Annunciation
44 *top right* Santiago. Cathedral.
Annunciation
45 *opposite* Castell' Arquato.
Church. Isaiah prophesies
Christ's birth
46 *right* Silos. Cloister. Visitation

the conversation which follows the Annunciation, and not simply the greeting.

Another confined space likely to bring Mary and Gabriel together is the side of an arch: carving in this position (which is generally described as an archivolt or voussoir) has access to much height but little width, and this must affect the way in which scenes are portrayed. A small pilgrim church at Villafranca del Bierzo, east of Santiago on the Pilgrim Route, shows a simple and calm Annunciation on its archivolt. In Santiago itself the Annunciation appears in the west portal on a trumeau (the vertical pillar between two doors); the carving here is more naturalistic, as one would expect from the fact that this portal was carved in 1188, and its beauty is nearer to the Gothic than to the Romanesque.

The Annunciation was celebrated on 25 March, nine months before Christmas Day; this was believed also to be the date of Christ's death, and the church additionally used it to commemorate Adam. It would be natural therefore, with so many themes clustering around the spring equinox, for the Fall and the Redemption, the tree of Paradise and the Cross, to be linked with the Annunciation. Such symbolism, bringing together a number of ideas central to the Christian

faith, was a favourite of monks and preachers, and it therefore formed part of the task given to carvers. But the limita-
tions of space make it unusual for Annunciation, Fall, and
Passion, all to be combined in one scene. Yet there are
echoes: for example, the thought of Mary as the new Eve
(just as Christ was the new Adam) was an important element in medieval theology. We have already seen one link,
on a Hildesheim door; and the apple which Mary sometimes holds in her hand probably refers back to Eve. It was
also thought significant that the angel's first word to Mary,
in Latin, was *Ave* – the reverse of Eva.

Symbolism of this kind is not very often developed in
carvings. Quite commonly, however, there is reference to
Christ's birth being the fulfilment of prophecy – a theme
which we should expect from the various links between the
Old and New Testaments that were discussed in the first
chapter. At Castell' Arquato, for example, Isaiah can be
seen holding a scroll which contains his prophecy[c] and
pointing to Mary as confirmation that it is now fulfilled.
The panel, which is less austere than earlier twelfth century
Italian work, is little-known: it is now the centrepiece of the
altar in the church of this hill-top town in North Italy, with
panels of the Annunciation and the Visitation on either side
of it.

This leads us to the second scene which precedes the
Nativity in a line of carvings, or even, as at Barcelona, occu-
pies another side of the Annunciation capital. It is the simple
one of two women meeting when Mary visits her cousin Elizabeth. There is also a warmer image (derived from Syrian
painting) of the two embracing, as at Silos, with Elizabeth
much the older of the two women (so stressing the miracle
of John the Baptist's birth). The more restrained Hellenistic
tradition, however, portrays Mary and Elizabeth as talking,
for this is the occasion of the Magnificat. The Visitation,
like the Annunciation, is an uncomplicated scene, easily
recognized.

The Nativity is not so straightforward. An early tradition
showed the miracle of Christ's birth without the near presence of either Mary or Joseph – but only of the ox and ass:
a carving at Gargilesse has such a scene. This may seem
strange, for the two animals are not mentioned in the gospels. Their presence derives not only from Luke's reference
to a manger but also from the early application to the scene

47 *above right* Gargilesse. Church. Nativity
48 *above* Santa Maria a Cerrate. Church. Nativity

of Isaiah's words[d] that 'the ox knows its owner, and the ass its master's crib'. Habakkuk[e] is also relevant, at least in some early texts: 'In the midst of two beasts shalt thou be known'. There is a charming wisdom in the expressions of the animals as they (closely followed by shepherds and wisemen) signify that the whole of creation marvels at this mystery of God incarnate.

The babe is usually shown wrapped tightly and lifted up, often on something resembling an altar; and this continues for many centuries, even when Mary is in the picture, as on a little-known carving at Santa Maria a Cerrate in Southern Italy. This depiction of the babe is an example of foreshadowing: Christ is to be the sacrifice, the bread laid on the

49 Estany. Cloister. Nativity

altar, the body laid in the tomb – with grave-clothes instead of swaddling-clothes. Only in much later times (and even then not in the Eastern church) does Mary look down lovingly on the babe in the representations that most people know best. In earlier Nativities, of which Estany provides a good example, Mary sleeps and Joseph watches while the animals nuzzle the babe above. The Protevangelium of James, which is to be found in the apocryphal gospels, tells a story about one Salome who came to the manger, doubting the Virgin Birth; this legend was repudiated later, and that may well account for her face having been obliterated on this capital. The same deliberate damage to a carving of this character can be seen on a portal at Vézelay.

To replace the story of Salome, and perhaps to match what pilgrims to Palestine were shown, the picture of a bath being prepared was often used, as in a panel from Bonannus' bronze doors at Pisa. The Byzantine tradition, on which he drew (though he used the technique of the German bronze-workers), regularly showed this bath: it stressed the humanity of Christ and foreshadowed his baptism. The cave here is another Eastern image: there were a number of caves around Bethlehem (and indeed the place shown there as Christ's birthplace is a cave); but there is reference also to the tomb of Christ's burial and his descent into Limbo for the Harrowing of Hell. The angels and shepherds above the cave make the panel at Pisa a most charming celebration of Incarnation and Redemption.

There are many lintels and doors which tell the whole Nativity story in successive scenes, as at Ferrara. The last of the three scenes here shows the animation of the shepherds: they are not said to have adored the child (as the wise men do in Matthew's gospel), but are usually shown receiving the news, as on a wooden panel in Cologne, and resolving to go to the manger. Like the wise men, they tend to be of different ages: young and old, simple and learned, come to the

50 *opposite* Pisa. Cathedral door. Nativity
51 *below* Ferrara. Cathedral. Nativity scenes

Incarnation. On a capital at Chauvigny the difference of ages is very marked. There is an Oriental air about these very unusual Chauvigny capitals – probably due to manuscript illustrations and ivory carvings imported from the East. The use of colour also strikes the eye. Many stone carvings show traces of polychromy, used either as adornment or to make the detail stand out. Since nearly all colour has now faded, it is easy for us to forget how bright the sculpture once looked; but other attempts to recreate the old effect, as in several churches near Clermont-Ferrand, have not been very successful.

The wise men of Matthew's gospel, sometimes referred to by the original name of Magi (which really means religious leaders or even astrologers), represent the heathen as the shepherds represent the Jews. The story of their coming to the manger has always intrigued the mind. In the Eastern church Christmas, on 6 January, was also Epiphany; this was a feast of light to celebrate God in Christ first being seen by the nations of the world, in the persons of the wise men. The western separation of the two feasts has given us 'the twelve days of Christmas'. But, for the carver, wise men came to the manger as early as shepherds. Very soon they became not wise men, or Magi, but kings: this was because Isaiah 60 and Psalm 72 were thought to prophesy their action. They also became three in number, because they gave three gifts, gold, frankincense and myrrh; these were traditional offerings to a king from the wealth and luxury of the East, but Christians held that they symbolized Christ's kingship, priesthood, and sacrifice. Names were given to the kings in due course; and, because they were prefigured by Noah's three sons, and were regarded as representing the three known continents, Europe, Africa and Asia, one of the kings in later times was portrayed as a Moor.

The little church of San Benito at Santiago shows the second king as black; but this can hardly have been part of the original concept, since the tradition was not current in Romanesque times, and the colouring must therefore have been added after the sculpture was first made. The second king is also often shown as the youngest of the three, as is evident on the sarcophagus of Dona Blanca at Najera. If there is any reference to the star, it is usually the second king who stands and points – but this feature, probably from a Nativity play, is not found in the earliest carvings.

52 *above* Santiago. San Benito church. Three kings worship
53 *below* Najera. Abbey church. Three kings worship

It is not easy to fit the scene of the three kings onto one capital, but it can be done. A capital at Lubersac shows this; but, as well as being crowded, it is rustic work, and the proportions are not pleasing. Far finer is the well-known capital at Autun, easy to study now that it is placed in the chapter house rather than in its original position. The child reaches out to touch the casket. Joseph, round the corner, is pensive, wondering at it all. His gesture, with hand on cheek, signified grief in early times; but for Joseph it sometimes means deep thought, sometimes detachment, sometimes weari-

ness. If the eyes are closed, it may even suggest the earlier dream which led him to accept the miracle of the Virgin Birth, or the dream which later urges him to go to Egypt.

We have seen that the coming of the Magi can be combined with other imagery. A striking tympanum at Neuilly-en-Donjon shows the three kings and Mary trampling underfoot the beasts which symbolize ancient evil[f]. Angels blow the trumpets of Judgment to signify that Christ is to defeat Satan. There is a beautiful rhythm in this carving, and a tall gracefulness which reminds some of El Greco. Even

54 *opposite, above* Autun. Cathedral. Three kings worship
55 *opposite, below* Autun. Cathedral. Joseph
56 *above* Neuilly-en-Donjon. Church. Three kings worship

[53]

57 *above* Toulouse. Musée des Augustins. Three kings worship
58 *below* Anzy-le-Duc. (now in museum of Paray-le Monial). Virgin and Child

57 more rhythmical is a badly damaged carving at Toulouse of the three kings' adoration. They advance in a kind of ballet. Here they are treading on Ionic capitals, and this suggests the ruin of old religion; their veiled hands are a gesture of reverence borrowed from the ceremonial art of the East. The surface of this sculpture is badly scarred; yet beneath the damage a most fluent composition appears.

58 It would be tempting to read a tympanum from Anzy-le-Duc as showing the three kings (who are sometimes depicted with the nimbus, since tradition held that they were later baptized by Thomas) being matched in forward-looking symbolism by the three women bringing spices to the tomb. Each group would then be flanked by a figure facing forward, and the unusual position of the babe on Mary's lap would then have reference to both groups of three, for it calls to mind the image which later became well-known as the Pietà. But the traditional explanation of this carving is simply that it shows the Virgin, amid saints, at the foot of a Christ in Glory – a scene which derives from an early fresco found at Bawit in Egypt. It is unusual, however, for obvious reasons, to see the babe with Mary when an adult Christ also appears, in scenes of Ascension or Glory. The illustrations in the fifth chapter bear this out.

During the twelfth century, as devotion to Christ's earthly life grew stronger, so the group of Mother and Child often stood alone, a subject not only for art but also for adoration. The worship of the kings was no longer an essential part of the scene, for the worshippers now were the faithful of the artist's own day. When depicted with the kings, Mary and her babe usually faced to the left of the viewer, looking at the kings as they approached; but, when the two of them were unaccompanied, an older Eastern style of art (which regularly showed the Virgin as 'Theotokos', or Mother of God) sometimes caused them to face forward. It was normal also to carve such images of Mother and Child in the round, as free-standing statues. Such representations became for succeeding ages some of the best-loved subjects for artist and sculptor.

Yet early Romanesque versions are not usually impressive. Mary tends to be treated as if she were simply the throne on which Christ sits, rather than as a person with deep humanity; and there is a solidity about the features and a total lack of tenderness which, though they inspired

strong devotion, make them less moving than the Gothic work of the following age. Yet sometimes, even in the starkest work, majesty redeems the lack of humanity: the tiny Spanish village of Covet, accessible only by a rough road, has a carving on the arch of the church which appeals, especially since Joseph is here included; he provides plenty of humanity.

At the end of the Romanesque period, the stiffness and heaviness of the early Madonnas give way to something more sensitive. Two contrasting carvings from northern Spain may make the point: one is in a natural cave in the abbey at Najera, and the other attracts many worshippers in the cathedral of Solsona. Devotion to the Virgin and Child meant that they were often shown receiving a special offering from contemporary Christians: in particular, a man of power would dedicate his church to them and be shown in the act of dedication. At Léon it is a monk who makes an offering of his church: he kneels in much the same attitude as the first of the three kings.

59 *top* Covet. Church. Virgin and Child
60 *above* Najera. Abbey church. Virgin and Child
61 *opposite* Solsona. Cathedral. Virgin and Child
62 *right* Léon. Cathedral museum. Virgin and Child, with monk

In the East there was a long tradition of refined work, particularly in painting. The solid and accomplished Roman style had been infused with the spirituality of less hard-headed peoples; this interaction with the east was reinforced by the wish to put a stronger emphasis on what is holy rather than on what is lifelike. The result was sometimes stiff and remote; but Romanesque art triumphed by blending the Byzantine emphasis on the sacred and eternal with the classical emphasis on portraying man realistically. Venice was an obvious meeting-place of East and West. In the cathedral of San Marco there is a marble relief of the Virgin standing alone and praying. The attitude of prayer is interesting: originally Christians prayed with the arms raised to heaven; but, when this was thought to be too like the pagan stance, the arms were held out horizontally, either as on the cross or (as here) in what is called the 'orans'

position, with the elbows bent, the forearms raised, and the palms turned outwards. The attitude of prayer that we know best, with the hands together, only became common in the twelfth century; and some have seen this as the spiritual equivalent of the homage ceremony, where a vassal kneels and places his hands, palm to palm, between the hands of his liege-lord.

Many Nativity sequences end with Luke's account of the Presentation in the Temple. 'Simeon received the boy', says the inscription in a delightful panel at Pisa; Anna can be seen giving thanks, with raised hand, behind him. These holy and expectant people saw in Jesus, before they died, the fulfilment of Israel's ancient hope of a Messiah. The occasion of this was the Purification of the Virgin, forty days after Jesus' birth[g]; in the Christian church the fortieth day after Christmas was celebrated as Candlemas, with a procession of lights. But the essence of the story is the offering of the child to the Temple, which Luke associates with the ransom of the first-born. This was accompanied by a sacrifice of two turtle doves or young pigeons, and Joseph can be seen holding these in one of the panels on the Hildesheim doors. Yet the emphasis here is rightly on Simeon

63 *opposite, left* Venice. Cathedral. Virgin
64 *opposite, right* Pisa. Cathedral door. Presentation
65 *above* Hildesheim. Cathedral door. Presentation

who, accepting the child, recognises his divinity and predicts his crucifixion. The placing of the figures is by no means uniform in this scene: yet another arrangement can be seen in a panel from Novgorod. The bronze panels of doors once again impress us by their absence of extraneous

detail. A few centuries later, these scenes will be so cluttered up with scenery and people that their force is lost. Romanesque art bothers little about the surroundings, but goes straight to the point.

Matthew's account of the Nativity follows the reactions of Herod to Christ's birth. The Magi are warned of Herod's wicked designs: a charming Romanesque convention, which can be seen on a capital at Tarragona, shows the three of them sleeping under a single blanket, and (an added discomfort) still wearing their crowns while they sleep. The angel here is thoroughly robust. But in the cloister of St. Trophime at Arles, and even more in the famous capital now in the chapter house at Autun, the angel has the gentle sweetness which befits a dream. The kings, we are told, re-

66 *right* Novgorod. Cathedral door. Presentation
67 *above* Tarragona. Cathedral cloister. Three kings sleep
68 *opposite* Autun. Cathedral. Three kings sleep

69 Estella. San Pedro church. Herod orders massacre

turned to their country by another way; some paintings suggest that they sailed home in three ships, but carvings do not pursue this theme.

Meanwhile Herod, in imperious form, as at Estella, orders his soldiers to kill. And kill they do: a simple panel at Pisa shows Herod giving his command, a soldier killing, and a mother grieving as she offers slight protection to the babe standing before her. The interest for the church of the story of the Massacre of the Innocents is that these are the first of many Christian martyrs, however little they may be thought to have volunteered for the post.

Such work as this, from France, Spain and Italy, reminds us that Romanesque art is an astonishingly successful mixture – and not only of the two traditions of Rome and Byzantium. We have seen that these two are representational, depicting figures and scenes with some concern for

70 Pisa. Cathedral door. Massacre of the Innocents

their appearance, and that the two techniques interacted, so that Byzantium spiritualized the Roman style and the West animated the Byzantine style. But there was another tradition, that of ornament and decoration: this was flowing and flexible, unhampered by appearances but relying only on geometry and linear movement. The Muslims practised this because they, like the Jews, felt that the divine was too holy to be portrayed; and, in the period of the iconoclasts, the Byzantine empire had similar doubts about work which might seem to encourage the worship of images. The ornamental style was also dear to the 'barbarians', whether from the East or from the North, and it left its mark even when these peoples were converted to Christianity. It might seem impossible to combine this tradition of ornament (which we in the West associate particularly with Celts and Scandinavians) and the other tradition, from Rome and Byzantium,

71 *above* Estany. Cloister. Flight into Egypt
72 *right* Autun. Cathedral. Flight into Egypt

of representing characters and scenes. But, with sculpture looked on as an adjunct to architecture, the decoration of capitals and portals was gradually suffused with the representation of animals and people; and figurative carving took over, on its surface, the spirals and patterns and desire to fill a whole space which had characterized the ornamental tradition. In harmonizing mass and representation on the one hand with ornament and fluidity on the other, no sculptors were more accomplished than those of Burgundy and of Languedoc (after its own rather massive effects had been lightened by Cluniac influence). The successful fusion of the two styles came originally from the ivory carvers who followed the patterns of the Utrecht Psalter (of the early ninth century); metal workers in Germany and Italy took it up; and the abbey of Cluny and its dependencies put the crowning touch on this unique blend of traditions.

73 Saulieu. Abbey church. Flight into Egypt

The final act of the Nativity story sees the Holy Family, warned by another dream, making its way to Egypt, as on a capital at Estany. The basis of the scene is a simple picture of Mary and the child sitting on an ass, with Joseph carrying the baggage. Joseph often walks in front of the donkey and looks resolutely ahead, as in a well-known capital at Autun; only in later centuries, when tenderness and human concern are more prominent, is the softer image more common as he turns back and looks with care and love on the Virgin and Child. The circles at the bottom of the Autun carving are clearly symbolic decoration. But in other carvings of the Flight, like that at Saulieu, they have sometimes been taken to be wheels; if they are, that is due to a memory of Passion plays in which a specially-constructed donkey was used. This device would figure in Christ's Entry into Jerusalem, a scene which is linked to the Flight not only by the ass but also by a palm-tree which often appears above Mary – as at Pisa. This palm-tree features in one of the many apocryphal stories which gathered round the Flight into Egypt: it was sought by the weary travellers for its shade and fruit, and it leant over because, according to the legend, Christ commanded it to do so for his mother's sake. So the Nativity story ends in repose and refreshment.

74 Pisa. Cathedral door. Flight into Egypt

3. Ministry

OUR LORD'S MINISTRY begins when John the Baptist recognizes the greater significance of Christ and baptizes him in the river Jordan[a]. Estany cloister has a simple and

75 Estany. Cloister. Baptism of Christ

direct picture of the scene, one of a series of capitals devoted to Christ's life. Wild landscape has small appeal in early medieval times (for love of Nature is a luxury usually reserved for those who no longer find natural forces a threat to peace of body and mind). The scenery therefore does not interest the carver; and the simplest way of representing the river Jordan is to make the water rise like a mound about Christ. This curious way of depicting the river may also be due to an early belief that the waters actually heaped themselves up around Christ, as they had piled themselves up when Joshua crossed the river; pilgrims to Palestine in the

76 Arezzo. Santa Maria church. Baptism of Christ

twelfth century saw a stone on the bank of the Jordan which was said to show how high the waters rose at the Baptism.

Other elements in the medieval carver's picture of the Baptism can also be seen at Estany. The dove, representing the Holy Spirit, descends from above in a vertical swoop. On the right is John, wearing a garment which suggests his rugged way of life in the wilderness. On the left is an angel, veiling his hands out of reverence (as we saw the Wise Men do). Later this veiling over the angels' hands was misunderstood, and the coverings were seen as clothes for Christ's emergence from the water. Each of the three figures in the Estany carving has a nimbus of light (a halo) around his head; this symbol is usually taken to signify sanctity, but its original message was that the wearer had a special power from God. The nimbus of Christ here, as often, has the cross within it.

Baptism in the Romanesque period was by immersion; for this reason Christ always stands in the water, and John,

77 Castle Frome. Church font. Baptism of Christ

instead of pouring water upon him, either takes his arm or places a hand on his head. A solemn carving at Arezzo shows the scene in a tympanum. Such tympana are rare in this part of the world, and this one is probably due to French influence in a region which lay on the usual pilgrim route to Rome. Here the dove too has a nimbus, to stress that it represents the Holy Spirit. Other interesting touches are the symbolic human soul in the mound of water (up which John seems to be climbing), and the different condition of the two trees behind Christ and John – a pictorial version of John's later words, 'He must increase, but I must decrease'[b].

But the Baptism is not only the start of Christ's ministry. It is also a new creation (the Holy Spirit above the waters being an obvious link with the Genesis story of the Creation[c]). It is a new birth for Christ: the words 'Thou art my son'[d] are followed in Psalm 2[e] by 'This day have I begotten thee'. It is also a new birth for humanity: Christ enters the waters, as mankind went into the Flood, and as the Israelites went through the Red Sea and later over Jordan; he comes forth from his Baptism victorious over sin. There is rich symbolism, therefore, for the carvers to draw on; and it can be seen in the place where one would expect baptisms to be carved – on a font.

The font at Castle Frome is unequalled in England. The movement and swirling decoration are balanced by an intense stillness in the faces. Like most of the Herefordshire work (which was discussed in the first chapter), it is fairly

78 *right, above* Castle Frome. Church font. St. Matthew
at Baptism
79 *right, below* Castle Frome. Church font. Creature
80 *above* Cologne. Sankt Maria im Kapitol, church door.
Baptism of Christ
81 *opposite* Liège. St. Bartholomew church. Baptism of
Christ

early, for it belongs to the first half of the twelfth century;
but it is certainly not primitive. Here we have the full Trin-
ity: both the hand of God and the dove of the Holy Spirit (of
which the head has been broken off) are visible above
Christ. Fishes swim in the water. On another part of the
font, a flying figure appears, surveying the scene: this is St.
Matthew pointing to his gospel, which is one of the three
which tell the story of Christ's Baptism. Below is the world
of wicked depths: the gloomy figures on the base may well
represent the sin which Christ has conquered. But when sin
has been defeated it more often takes the form of lions,
dragons and serpents, such as were seen on the portal of

Neuilly-en-Donjon. A Baptism from the doors of Sankt Maria im Kapitol, Cologne, also has a fine fury of beasts being trodden underfoot, to denote the conquest of sin.

Another beautful font, at Liège, shows a Baptism very different in style. This font is of bronze, in which Northern Europe had a longer tradition of supple work than it had in stone. The sculptor has a sureness of touch derived from Classical carving; but he also derives from other sources a spiritual depth which raises this work far above mere realism – indeed the font looks forward to Gothic forms rather than back to Roman. All the scenes are finely composed and expressively carved. Exquisite also are the oxen on the base;

82 Hildesheim. Cathedral font. Baptism of Christ

I   Gerona. Cathedral cloister. Annunciation

II Barcelona. Cathedral. Visitation

III Cologne. Sankt Maria im Kapitol, church door. The shepherds

IV   Chauvigny. Church of St. Peter. The shepherds

V Lucca. Cathedral. Volto Santo

VI   Barcelona. Museum of Catalan Art. Majestad

VII   Cologne. Diocesan Museum. Crucifix

VIII   S. Juan de las Abadesas. Monastery. Head of Christ

the origin of these is the sea of brass which King Solomon ordered for the temple[f], beneath which three oxen looked out to each of the four points of the compass.

The great font at Hildesheim has different supporters (which do not appear in this illustration) – figures pouring the waters of salvation from jars: they are the four rivers of Paradise, and above them are four virtues, four prophets, and symbols of the four evangelists. On this side of the font we see that the waters of the Jordan still, in the middle of the thirteenth century, have the unnatural look of a small mound covering Christ's nakedness; and John the Baptist, improbably, still climbs up the waters to reach and baptize Christ. On the other sides of the font, the three scenes are of 'types' of Baptism; among these is Moses crossing the Red Sea, which has already been shown.

Romanesque carving, like the sculpture of the ancient Greeks, is closely related to the architecture of which it forms a part. Whereas the Greeks fitted their scenes on a triangular pediment or a square metope, the medieval carvers had to fit theirs on a round tympanum or capital: the effect of this on the composition is obvious. But a font allows more space, although not all scenes can there be viewed simultaneously. So does a lintel, the length of which invites a series of pictures. Lintels on the doors of Baptisteries are very suitable for portraying Christ's baptism; and here the event is often part of the life not of Christ but of John the Baptist. An interest in John's role sometimes results in a scene of Christ blessing him, as at Parma, while both men stand in the water.

The later story of John the Baptist's life also appears on this lintel at Parma. These later events are most clearly seen

83 *below* Parma. Baptistery. Christ blesses John

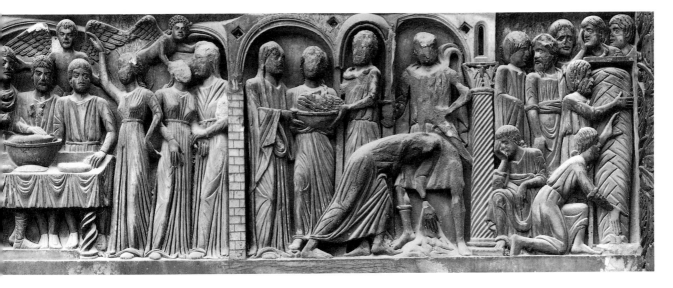

at Pisa, where the baptistery again has a lintel which concerns itself with John. In the third scene here he is arrested for his rebuke to Herod Antipas[g]. On the extreme right, the beheading of John and the care of his corpse by his disciples are seen. In the fourth scene, Herodias and Salome are talking together on the right of the picture, under the inspiration of a wicked demon who is putting malicious thoughts into their minds. Between them and the feast of Herod is a scene which gave good scope for the worldlier imaginations of the carver – the dance of Salome, which led to the execution of John. The great column at Hildesheim, which, like the doors, is Ottonian work dating from the beginning of the eleventh century, gives a most vivid picture of Salome dancing, though her expression would not have appealed to Oscar Wilde or Richard Strauss.

The portrait of Herod himself sometimes has great dignity, as on a capital at Ferrara. But in other carvings he knows that his role in all this is not very dignified: there seems to be a certain mixture of desire and shame as he grants her request to Salome in the attractive and human sculpture which can be seen at Toulouse. The drapery here has most decorative curves: these are an interesting feature

84 *top* Pisa. Baptistery. Life of John the Baptist
85 *opposite, far left* Hildesheim. Column of Bernward. Dance of Salome
86 *opposite, left* Ferrara. Cathedral museum. Herod feasts
87 *right* Toulouse. Musée des Augustins. Herod and Salome

of some Languedoc sculpture. The same patterns are also to be seen further north; perhaps the most striking examples are at Vézelay. This decorative element in Romanesque sculpture comes, as we have seen, from the North and the East: its linear effect adds movement and animation to the solid and immobile tradition of some earlier sculpture.

The final event of John the Baptist's life is well shown on another capital which is now in the Musée des Augustins at Toulouse. These capitals of John's death are particularly well preserved: in this one a graceful Salome can be seen passing something up to the table – it is a head which, luckily for the sensitive, is not carved with much precision.

Immediately after the Baptism of Christ comes the story of his Temptation; this was presumably told to the disciples by Our Lord in the vivid pictorial form of which Matthew and Luke give the fullest versions[h]. The theme is a fascinating one: the temptations, which are not the ones which assail man, follow Old Testament expectations of what the Messiah might do with his power – feed the hungry by magical means, seize worldly dominion, or dazzle onlookers with a purposeless miracle. It is easy perhaps for the Christian to suppose that their rejection was easy; yet Jesus, being fully human, must have found it very tempting both to test the powers of which his Baptism had given him a new awareness and to settle on a mission which would sensationally change the world. It is understandable, therefore, that in later ages many artists should depict Satan as an insidious tempter, charming and plausible with his offer of attractive options which might well have prevailed over the

88 *above* Toulouse. Musée des Augustins. Herod feasts
89 *opposite, top left* Autun. Cathedral. Temptation of Christ
90 *opposite, top right* Saulieu. Abbey church. Temptation of Christ
91 *opposite, below* Plaimpied. Church. Christ and the Tempter

much more difficult choice of love and suffering. For medieval man, however, the fight between good and evil was so clear-cut that it had to be starkly portrayed; and so the tempter in Romanesque carvings is generally a foul and grotesque figure, more suggestive of beast than of man.

The repulsive ferocity of Satan contrasts with the calmness of Christ in a vivid carving at Autun: this shows the temptation which urged Christ to leap down from a pinnacle of the temple. Surprisingly, perhaps, it is the devil who stands on the pinnacle, while an angel with drawn sword gives support to Our Lord – a memory of the gospel statement that 'angels came and ministered unto him' and a feature which may also remind us of the Archangel Michael's battle with Satan. There is even more monstrous villainy in the devil who at Saulieu tempts Christ to turn a stone into bread; but here Christ dominates the scene as he points to an open book and calmly confounds the devil by quoting the scriptures.

Another carving which concentrates on the rejection by Christ of Satan's temptations can be seen on a capital at Plaimpied. The style of this sculpture, with its elongated face, circular lines, and lively movement, is reminiscent of

the fluid work at Toulouse and Vézelay which has just been discussed. But it also bears a striking resemblance to the very beautiful capitals which were made for Nazareth. It is clear that French sculptors of the twelfth century moved not only down the pilgrim routes to Santiago and Rome but also to patrons in the Holy Land, where the crusades had recently given a stimulus to the making of pilgrimages and the building of churches.

For a final scene of the Temptation, it is worth looking once more at the Pisa door. Here we see a most placid rejection of Satan: Christ is seated on a high mount, over against the temple, and a very docile devil stands attentively before him.

Jesus' first miracle, which is, for doctrinal reasons, more often represented than any other, is the turning of water into wine at Cana in Galilee[i]. In the words of a famous conceit, 'Nympha pudica Deum vidit et erubuit' (The modest water saw its God and blushed). This is a complicated scene, difficult to fit into the limited space available to the sculptor. In this it resembles the Last Supper, which it was believed to foreshadow. The parallel is between the changing of water into wine and the changing of wine into the blood of Christ. At Charlieu, a curved table makes it possible to fit the whole scene into a lovely but disordered tympanum. The wine-cup in Christ's hand underlines the resemblance; but the two men with their large jars at the side of the picture indicate that this is indeed Cana. On the arch above, there is a Transfiguration scene, with the figures in sweet movement: we can see from the quality of this carving that the damage to heads in the Cana scene below has been particularly sad. More of the symbolic meaning of the miracle is suggested on the column at Hildesheim: there is both remoteness and loving authority in the strong figure of Christ, as he looks out with an invitation to the believer and at the same time turns the water to wine.

This Hildesheim column is unique in the full picture it provides of the events of Christ's ministry. In general, Romanesque art picks out one or two scenes only, valued for their special significance, and depicts these; we have nothing that resembles an illustrated gospel apart from this column, which follows the Roman tradition of commemorating an emperor by successive scenes of his triumphs. The church's calendar also played a part in focusing the

attention of worshippers, and so of carvers, on particular events, especially at the beginning and end of Christ's life. It therefore set limits to the story, just as the evangelists (who offer, of course, nothing like a full biography of Christ) had earlier recorded for the sake of significance rather than completeness. Christmas, Passion Week, Easter, and Whitsuntide, dominated the church's year; these, together with the Eucharist, were the chief elements in what believers heard in the liturgical services. It is not surprising that other events and miracles and parables were less important in the sculptor's repertoire of subjects than the great mysteries of Incarnation and Redemption.

The apostle Peter was important, however, both to Rome and to Cluny, which was closely connected with the Pope; so, when scenes of Christ's ministry are illustrated, Peter often plays a prominent part in them. Hardly ever in medieval carvings is he handed the keys – though this is a scene which underpinned Papal claims to primacy and which therefore one might expect. He does, however, receive a

92 *opposite, top* Pisa. Cathedral door. Temptation of Christ
93 *above* Charlieu. Abbey church. Marriage feast at Cana
94 *opposite, below* Hildesheim. Column of Bernward. Marriage feast at Cana

[79]

special blessing in a scene at Much Wenlock: this shows the calling of the disciples[j] – and not, as has sometimes been claimed, Christ walking on the water. Peter is sitting in the bows of the lower boat, and his outstretched hand is clasped by Our Lord. Above him, in the other boat, the youthful John can be seen. The 'steerboard', which is on the starboard side, as it should be, is handled by Andrew in the lower and by James in the higher boat.

The meeting of Christ with the woman of Samaria at the well[k] had some appeal in early times: the living water hinted at baptism; and Christians who were not Jews must have welcomed the story of a Gentile woman receiving such teaching from Christ, and coming towards a recognition of him as the Messiah. This event is depicted on the Hildesheim column with the simple strength which marks all the scenes that appear on it. Nobody knows what is represented in the next illustration – a fine fragment in Uppingham church; indeed, few people know the carving at all. I like to find in it an echo of the line in the 'Dies Irae' which moved

Dr. Johnson so profoundly – 'Quaerens me sedisti lassus' (It was in search of me that you sat there weary) – and to read it as Christ resting by the well in Samaria, tired indeed but still alert to meet human need and doubt.

Another scene with a woman which appealed to the carvers was the washing of Christ's feet. The gospel accounts of this event vary. Matthew[l] and Mark[m] say that Christ was at supper with a certain Simon, and that his head was anointed. Luke[n] says that the woman was a sinner, and the occasion is used for Christ's teaching on forgiveness. For him and for John[o] the feet are anointed, and this is the tradition that the carvers follow. John alone names the woman, telling us that she was Mary, the sister of Martha. But she is usually identified in medieval times as Mary Magdalene, perhaps because memories of both Luke's and John's accounts have been run together. A moving portrayal of this scene can be found in Gloucestershire at Leonard Stanley. The figures are rather primitive, and Christ's hand stretched out in blessing is disproportionate; but, thanks to the confines of the capital, the ancient posture of a guest at table, lying on a couch rather than sitting on a chair, is faithfully presented. There is also a small fragment, preserved in the church at Toller Fratrum, which seems to be of this scene;

the loss of the rest is particularly sad since the sculpture has some affinity with the two wonderful works at Chichester described at the end of this chapter. Outside the church of Santa Maria at Uncastillo a mysterious and emotional carving appears as one element in a rich and varied façade. This could well represent Our Lord's loving forgiveness of the sinner. Both the Toller Fratrum and Uncastillo carvings should be compared for style with an interesting fragment

95 *opposite, top left* Much Wenlock. Lavabo. Christ calls the Apostles
96 *opposite, top right* Hildesheim. Column of Bernward. Christ and the woman of Samaria
97 *opposite, below* Uppingham. Church. Seated figure
98 *above* Leonard Stanley. Church. Christ's feet are washed
99 *left* Toller Fratrum. Church. Christ's feet are washed
100 *below* Uncastillo. Santa Maria church. Christ's feet are washed

101 *top* Modena. Museo Civico. Mary Magdalene swoons
102 *above* Pisa. Cathedral door. Transfiguration

in the museum at Modena: this in fact represents Mary Magdalene swooning at the tomb of Christ, an incident almost certainly taken from a Passion play.

A most significant event in Christ's ministry, shortly before he sets out for Jerusalem, is the Transfiguration[P]. This is a sign of Christ's fulfilment of the Law and the Prophets, and also (according to Luke) a prediction of the Passion of Christ. A fluent representation of this scene has been shown on the arch at Charlieu above the tympanum devoted to the miracle at Cana in Galilee. It also appears on cathedral doors: a good example is a panel by Bonannus at Pisa. The Transfiguration was a favourite scene in mosaics — the monastery at Sinai has a fine early example — but it is rather less common than one might expect in early Romanesque stone carvings. This is partly because the Transfiguration was not generally commemorated in the West until the late middle ages, and partly also because its general pattern was often taken over by a Christ in Glory or a Christ of the Last Judgment. However, the tympanum at Charité-sur-Loire, which shows some affinity with the Ile de France sculptures, is unmistakably a Transfiguration. Christ stands in a 'mandorla' (an oval-shaped expression of surrounding light, which indicates the glory of Christ on very special occasions). Moses and Elijah stand on either side of him. Veiled hands again indicate the awe and amazement of the

disciples; but Peter, on the left, the practical man of the three, whose instinct is always to act (sometimes even before thinking), will soon be proposing the building of three tabernacles. Below the tympanum the sculptor has illustrated two other scenes in which Christ's divine glory is revealed.

The parables of Jesus might seem to offer great scope for the carver of narrative scenes; yet those who study Romanesque sculpture have to think very hard to recall any such work. The events through which salvation came to man, and the symbolism used by contemporary preachers, mattered more to the medieval church than the stories told by

103 Charité-sur-Loire. Abbey church. Transfiguration

104 Moissac. Abbey church. Dives and Lazarus

Jesus himself. The two most famous parables of all, the Prodigal Son and the Good Samaritan, are hardly ever illustrated – though a capital at Autun almost certainly represents the father putting a robe on the prodigal son.

Stories of forgiveness and mercy do not seem to have appealed as much in medieval iconography as those parables which gave dire warnings. The miser, often shown suffering the torments of the damned, could caution people against trusting in riches, as well as giving great cheer to the many who lacked riches. It is natural therefore that he should bring to mind the story of Dives and Lazarus[q]. The superb portal at Moissac shows the rich man feasting heartlessly on the right. The story now moves to the left – away from the doors. In the centre the dogs lick Lazarus' sores; then, above him, an angel carries off his soul. Next we see Abraham holding the soul of Lazarus in his bosom. But the figure on the extreme left, holding a scroll, raises a question. He has been identified by various scholars (T.S.R. Boase, for example, and Raymond Rey) as St. Luke or a second patriarch or Simeon. But it seems to me far more likely that the carving follows the parable to its conclusion: it must surely show a leaner Abraham, here with no capacious bosom, teaching the final lesson – that Moses and the prophets should be enough, without any miraculous return by Dives from the dead, to warn men against his fate.

105 Aulnay. Church. Wise and foolish Virgins

An even more general warning was supplied by the parable of the Wise and Foolish Virgins[r]. For they told everyone, rich and poor, to be ready for a day of judgment which might come at any moment, and which would separate the saved and the damned in the sharpest possible way. A play with this theme was performed in medieval times at Limoges; and it was the west of France which took up the story most eagerly. Aulnay has a splendid portal which includes the Wise and Foolish Virgins. The churches in Poitou and Saintonge, of which Aulnay is one, feature less in this book than their counterparts in the east of France for one particular reason: the carvings in this area, though finely executed, are usually on the archivolts themselves (that is to say, on the under-curves of the arches) rather than on tympana. There is therefore scope for a series of figures, one above the other, rather than a scene. So the subjects tend to be secular, or purely ornamental, and biblical events are not often shown. But the Wise and Foolish Virgins can be placed in a line that fits an archivolt – as can the Elders of the Apocalypse, who will be discussed in chapter 5. The portal of a church is a powerfully appropriate place for reminding the worshipper who enters that it is literally of vital import whether the day of doom shows him or her prepared, with a full lamp, or unprepared, with an empty one.

The miracles shown in the carvings are usually those of

healing. Christ, with his power over Nature and sin, could be looked to for removing weaknesses of body and spirit. There is great dignity and power in a scene of healing from that great column at Hildesheim which has already provided so many examples of the sculptor's skill. Another healing took place, according to Mark and Luke[s], without a conscious decision by Jesus: a woman with an issue of blood touched his garment in the crowd and was immediately cured. Even when the disciples said that one person could not be singled out when the crowd was pressing all around, Jesus insisted that someone had touched him and been healed. The woman then came forward and confessed. A scene from the Hildesheim column graphically shows the woman kneeling in fear and a stern Christ turning to praise her faith and to confirm the miracle.

The greatest of miracles is, of course, the raising of the dead. And among the very greatest works of Romanesque sculpture are the two stone panels at Chichester which show the raising of Lazarus[t]. This event foreshadows Christ's own resurrection just a week later, and serves also as a symbol of spiritual rebirth. The mingled power and tenderness of the two Chichester sculptures are most striking. In the first panel Christ arrives at Bethany, which is pictured as having a city gate; there Martha and Mary greet him. He strides ahead of his disciples. Their faces show the resolu-

106 *above, right* Hildesheim. Column of Bernward. Healing miracle
107 *above* Hildesheim. Column of Bernward. Healing miracle
108 *opposite* Chichester. Cathedral. Christ's arrival at Bethany

109. Chichester. Cathedral. Raising of Lazarus

tion required to go up to Jerusalem, and we recall Thomas's bold saying, 'Let us go also that we may die with him'. The expressions also reveal the grief which was felt at Lazarus' death: this is the occasion when we are told that Jesus wept. In the second panel Christ raises Lazarus from his grave. Sadness, rather than amazement, is still the predominant note. Martha and Mary here play only a small part, while Peter looses the bands of Lazarus; one gravedigger clenches his teeth with effort. The size of the figures is mainly governed by the 'spiritual perspective', which requires that the most important characters be shown as the largest. It is said that more than one sculptor worked on these two panels. It is also said that French, German, and Scandinavian influences can be detected: for comparison, the Deposition at Externsteine, shown later, is perhaps the most similar to Chichester in style of all the foreign carvings displayed in this book. But, whatever the influences and whoever was responsible for this noble English work, the intensity of the expressions, and the strong sense of divine power, make it a uniquely impressive picture of the last action of Christ's ministry before Passion week.

4. Passion

PASSION WEEK, which ends with disaster and degradation in human terms, begins with a worldly triumph: Christ's Entry into Jerusalem is described by all four evangelists[a] as a procession full of glory and excitement. 'Blessed be he that cometh in the name of the Lord' is one of the verses which end the Hallel[b], a group of Psalms that were recited at the great Jewish feasts, expressing the Messianic hope. The verses were accompanied by the waving of palm branches; and it may be that this celebration underlay the reception which Jesus received. The prophecy of Zechariah[c], to which Matthew and John draw attention, does of course stress the humility as well as the triumph of the Saviour; and the riding of an ass, rather than a horse, strongly confirms this element of the scene. Nevertheless, the entry has echoes of the conqueror coming home in triumph to his own capital: and this was strengthened by the fact that in medieval times Jerusalem was thought of as the heavenly city, and not only the earthly one.

In Palm Sunday processions the people of the Middle Ages took the opportunity to rejoice and celebrate, between the rigours of Lent and the sorrows of the Passion. Such processions often used full-scale wooden models of the donkey, with Christ as rider, and some of these have survived. Their wheels, as we have already seen at Saulieu, also feature at times in carvings of the Flight into Egypt. Depictions of the Entry into Jerusalem, however, tend to be more sophisticated. A Pisa panel of the scene is very lifelike. It has 'The Day of Palms' as its inscription; and, in addition to the palm branch carried by a disciple, palms can be seen growing in a strange, contorted way from the city walls, while scribes and Pharisees peer out apprehensively from among them. At Pisa, as elsewhere, the carvings usually show that garments, rather than palm-branches, are being strewn beneath the donkey's feet. Yet the emphasis of the medieval procession would have been on what the crowds carried, rather than on what was laid on the ground before the ass.

The carrying of palm-branches – a dominant element in John's account of the Entry – is a feature of a tympanum at

110 Pisa. Cathedral door. Christ's entry into Jerusalem

Pompierre. The movement is from right to left; and the disciples with their palm-branches follow Jesus rather stiffly. There is also a second smaller donkey behind the one on which Christ rides: this shows that the carver was following Matthew's account of Palm Sunday, since Matthew seems to misunderstand a Hebrew idiom in Zechariah's prophecy and writes as though there were two animals in the procession. Above this Entry there are various scenes from the Nativity: at the top, the Flight into Egypt shows Mary riding on a camel; this is surprising, since we should expect to see her on a donkey, matching the scene below.

A tympanum at Aston Eyre portrays Christ himself holding a palm-branch, which is a token sometimes of martyrdom and not solely of triumph. The need for a strictly frontal view of Our Lord means that the riding is awkwardly carved; this position would have been easier in the East, where Christ was regularly shown riding side-saddle, as can be seen on an ivory in the British Museum. But the carver had no problem with profiles: he touches the heart with the old man sitting on the ground, his branches held out before him, and with the sweet air of satisfaction and surprise on the face of the donkey, who has been stretched out to fill the tympanum. A famous poem by G.K. Chesterton ('When fishes flew and forests walked . . .'), and a fine sermon by Dom Bernard Clements, which has been reprinted and copied by others, take the same line as the carver and give particular attention to the humble ass.

The events and teaching of the next few days fill many pages of the gospels. For the carver, however, the story hurries on to the last twenty-four hours. Judas agrees to betray his master for thirty pieces of silver[d]: a relief inside the cathedral at Modena shows Caiaphas and his treasurer preparing to pay him. The carver cannot resist tracing the pen-

111 *above* Pompierre. Church. Christ's entry into Jerusalem
112 *opposite, above* Aston Eyre. Church. Christ's entry into Jerusalem
113 *opposite, below* Modena. Cathedral. Judas and Caiaphas

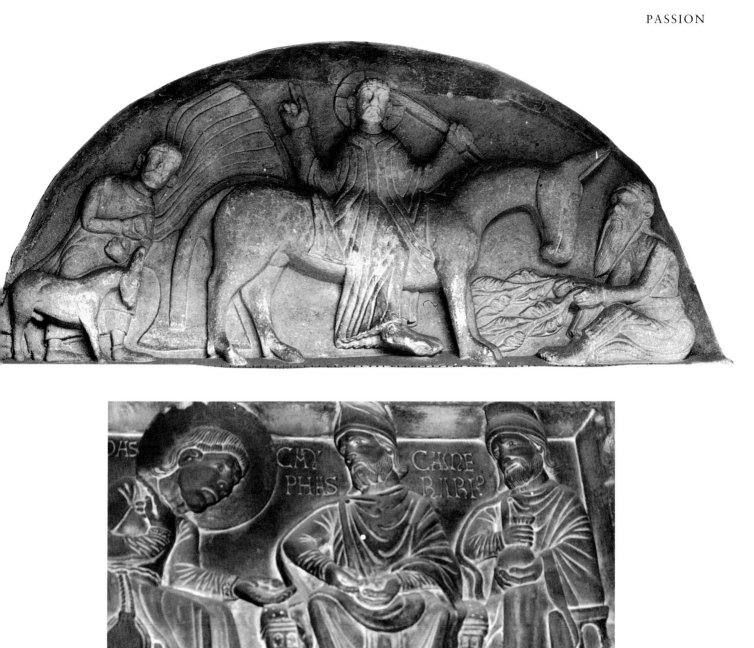

sive doubt of Judas during the transaction, and he even gives him the nimbus, or halo, which is usually reserved for those with the supernatural power and glory of saints.

The Last Supper[e] was bound to be a crucial subject for Christian carvers. It had central importance in explaining Christ's sacrifice on the cross: it also looked ahead, through the institution of the New Covenant, to the great service celebrated in the Church – the Eucharist (thanksgiving) or communion with Christ by the eating of bread and drinking of wine. (Other views of the significance of this service are not much reflected in the names given to it – 'Mass', for example, having no meaning except that the service ends with the words *Ite, missa est*). If any food is shown on the table, apart from the bread, it is more often fish than the paschal lamb. This is partly because loaves and fishes were used in the Feeding of the Multitude[f], which was sometimes linked by preachers to the Last Supper. But a more important reason is that the fish had long been a symbol of Christ, because of an early acronym: the initials of 'Jesus Christ, Son of God, Saviour' spelt the Greek word for fish. Even the bread which is mentioned in the gospels is less often shown than the cup, which seemed to offer clearer symbolism of the coming sacrifice. It is only in more recent times that the full theme of taking, blessing, breaking, and sharing (which is central to the gospel accounts and to St. Paul's even earlier record) has had its full significance for most believers.

The identifying of Judas as the traitor is also a feature of portrayals of the Last Supper. Whereas Eastern artists use Matthew's account, Western art often follows the narrative of John's gospel (which was the favourite one in the medieval liturgy) and shows Jesus handing the sop to Judas. This is a complicated scene, especially as Judas cannot have the place on Jesus' right or left, since these naturally belong to Peter and to John, the beloved disciple. For a panel of a bronze door, such as that in Verona, there is no great problem. Even so, the carver of this rough but sensitive panel has only managed to fit in eight disciples.

Stone carving is more difficult still. We have seen already that Romanesque sculpture belongs to its architecture in an intimate way, and also inherits an ornamental tradition. This means that a scene normally has just two possible sites, since the archivolt only allows a series of figures climbing up an arch. One of these sites is the capital at the top of a

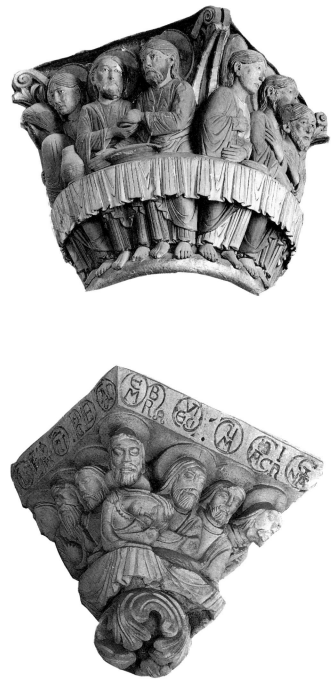

column. In ancient times these capitals were purely decorative; but the later styles, known as Corinthian and
Byzantine, came over the years to have figures and plants in-
serted in the ornamentation. So capitals became convenient
places for the display of Biblical scenes; but they are of
course confined spaces, and liable to introduce distortion.
They often have marked rhythm and eloquence, but there is
little room for a scene that demands width or includes many
figures. Nevertheless, there are some representations of the
Last Supper on capitals – at Issoire, for example. The shared
meal receives the main emphasis here; and on the far side of
this capital Judas reaches across to dip his hand with Jesus
in the dish – the sign which, according to Matthew, reveals
him as the traitor. On other capitals the emphasis is upon
John, the beloved disciple, who leant on Jesus' bosom at the
Last Supper. He is shown on a capital at Lugo, with a line of
dignified faces above him. But the disadvantage of putting a
large scene on a capital remains: because there is so little
breadth, one can only see it all by looking at different sides
in succession. It is not surprising therefore that most

114 *top, left* Verona. S. Zeno, church door. Last Supper
115 *top, right* Issoire. Church. Last Supper
116 *below* Lugo. Cathedral. Last Supper

[93]

117 Dijon. Museum. Last Supper

capitals concentrate on the supper itself and do not add to the difficulty by trying to include the exposure of Judas across the table.

The other natural site for carving is the tympanum: this, being radial in its general effect, produces another distortion, and tends, like the Greek pediment, to compress the outer figures. On a tympanum from St. Bénigne, Dijon, the artist has contrived to make an interesting picture, with Christ dominating the table, with John leaning his head upon Christ, and with a diminutive Judas receiving the sop on the far side of the table. Whereas at Charlieu the table was curved, this one is straight, so increasing the geometrical problem; even though the carver has imposed a terrible shrinkage on the outer figures, there is no room for all the disciples.

For a full presentation of the Last Supper, such as was possible in paintings, we have to look to the few rectangles that are available. One is the lintel, which usually contains a succession of scenes. The other is the frieze outside the church, less closely related to the architecture. The little-known church at Vouvant has such a frieze; and so we see

there one of the most complete carvings of the Last Supper. Judas clutches his money-bag, Peter his key. Other disciples suggest dignitaries of the church in a manner that would not be found in earlier carvings.

John's gospel does not record the taking of the bread and wine, though significantly he makes the Last Supper the occasion of Christ's words about the True Vine. But John does begin this part of his narrative with the account of Jesus washing the disciples' feet. This washing is a gesture of humility, a token of the love enjoined by the New Commandment, and a·sign of the forgiveness of sins. It has therefore many of the overtones of the institution of the Eucharist. It also had its own link with a rite of the church, in which feet were washed; echoes of this element in the liturgy lingered on in the services held on Maundy Thursday. A capital at Autun shows Christ washing Peter's feet; and the angel holding a towel behind Christ seems to be playing the

118 *above* Vouvant. Church. Last Supper
119 *bottom, left* Autun. Cathedral. Christ washes the disciples' feet
120 *bottom, right* Estany. Cloister. Christ washes the disciples' feet

part which a deacon in the medieval ceremony would have played. It is not easy to show Peter's successive reactions – first the refusal and then the insistence on having head and hands washed too. Sometimes, as at Autun, he raises his hand to decline Christ's service; sometimes he points eagerly to his head. The sculptor at Estany, however, makes no attempt to follow Peter's gestures: he simply recalls that Peter will shortly deny his master, and portrays him in an attitude of grief, while Christ ministers to him as a healer.

The Agony in the Garden[g] is an event that has strong echoes for Christians who wrestle with the problem of pain and suffering in the world. Yet there are not many representations of it in the early medieval period. The doors of Benevento cathedral (sadly wrecked in the Second World War) include a fine portrayal of this scene. The intensity of Christ's prayer is well conveyed. Above him the angel of the Agony leans attentively downwards. Only in later times would the angel be shown actually holding the cup of which Christ's prayer makes mention.

A more popular scene in the Romanesque period was the betrayal and arrest of Christ[h]. This had been shown from earliest times: the dramatic element clearly appealed strongly to the carvers. A frieze at St. Gilles du Gard, probably derived from manuscripts, shows the scene of Judas' kiss graphically. But the Roman tradition in Provence was strong, and here a heavy realism seems to take precedence over a special Romanesque feature, the expressing of an internal, rather than an external, truth. The only figure displaying strong feeling is the soldier immediately behind Our Lord. Further along the same frieze, an impassive Peter has seized the servant of the High Priest, in the rear of the soldiers, and is parting him from his ear with surgical precision. The victim has feelings, but they are obvious ones.

Very different in its spirit is the arrest of Christ seen on a door at Verona. Here the figures, for all the menace, seem to perform a carefully-composed dance. Italy, in spite of its Roman heritage, was more open than Provence to Byzantium and to Germany, to the spiritual quality of man and the movement of the metal-worker's art. There is therefore a certain lyrical quality in the structure of this panel, and in the calm, superhuman readiness of Jesus to accept his arrest, even though the actual carving is less sophisticated than that on the frieze at St. Gilles du Gard.

121 *top left*
Benevento.
Cathedral door.
Agony in the Garden
122 *right* St. Gilles du Gard.
Abbey church.
Arrest of Christ
123 *above* St. Gilles du Gard.
Abbey church.
Peter and Malchus
124 *bottom left* Verona.
S. Zeno, church door.
Arrest of Christ

A contrasting picture of the Arrest can be seen on one of the two Benevento panels which show the scene. Here the power of Christ is the dominant theme, as the carver takes up John's statement that Judas and the band of soldiers drew back and fell to the ground.

Christ's trial before the Sanhedrin is rarely portrayed in the Middle Ages. But during this trial Peter is present, having followed Christ still, though at a distance. His denial of his master[j] forms the subject of a vivid stone relief in Modena cathedral. Peter warms large hands and feet before the fire; the servant girl takes one hand from her work to point accusingly at Peter; and between them is the cock, just about to crow. There were times later when the carvers concentrated on Peter as the forerunner of the Pope, and indicated his power, signified by the keys of the kingdom, rather than the weakness and shame of his denial. Churches called 'St. Peter at Cock-crow' tend to be early ones. The story of his denial was not forgotten, however: it was good for the sinner to know that even the foremost of the disciples had need of penitence and forgiveness.

Christ is then taken before Pilate[j]. In a panel at Hildesheim he has the distinctive head which is the mark of this artist. He is led by two servants, one of whom seems about to strike him, into Pilate's presence. The temptation assailing Pilate is indicated by a small dragon on his left-

125 *above* Benevento. Cathedral door. Arrest of Christ
126 *above, right* Modena. Cathedral. Peter's denial
127 *opposite* Hildesheim. Cathedral door.
Christ before Pilate

hand side: occasionally this is balanced by the figure of Pilate's wife, or a messenger from her, urging him to be careful. But Pilate's dilemma and doubt are more often indicated by the dramatic moment in which he is seen washing his hands.

The stations of the Cross, leading the mind gradually up to Calvary, were a later series of devotional images. In Romanesque times the story usually moves straight on to the Crucifixion itself[k]. It is sometimes said that the early Christians shrank from showing Christ on the cross, since crucifixion remained a most degrading punishment for criminals in the Roman empire, and that they used symbols only. But veneration of the cross, particularly after Constantine's mother, Helena, claimed during her visit to Jerusalem in the early fourth century to have discovered the true cross, meant that this inevitably became the central image of the Christian faith for succeeding ages. It is true that the triumph of Christ, rather than his acute suffering, was the dominant theme in the early Middle Ages: only later did meditation on the horrors of the Passion lead to greater prominence being given to the agony of Our Lord.

Some of the finest Romanesque portrayals of the Crucifixion therefore show Christ in a long sleeved robe, with a distinctive knotted belt, rather than with a loincloth or naked. In origin, this was probably the exalted Christ of the Second Coming[1], with the arms stretched out straight in the ancient attitude of prayer and only symbolically nailed to the cross. Far the most influential of such images was the famous 'Volto Santo' at Lucca, said by legend to have been carved by Nicodemus; this was well known in the eleventh century, and indeed William Rufus used to swear by it. Similar images are to be found in places other than Lucca, especially in and around Barcelona, where the museums possess the finest collection of Romanesque crucifixes to be seen anywhere. These Catalonian crucifixes were known by the name 'Majestad', which emphasises their purpose – to show Christ reigning from the cross, rather than suffering. Their serene dignity and presence are striking, and some of them, like the 'Volto Santo', retain their vivid colouring. All show the two feet separately, not nailed to the cross – indeed the later image of the two feet together, pierced by one nail, at first raised objections from believers who were accustomed to the 'Majestad'.

The tradition of a robed Christ lingered on, as can be seen at Cologne, even when the carver made more attempt to show Christ in a hanging position. But, in places where this tradition was not known, the robed figure with a beard was puzzling. It was assumed to be a woman, and she became a legendary saint, with the name of St. Wilgefortis (perhaps a corruption of Virgo Fortis). The story was that, urged by her father to marry an unwanted suitor, she prayed for the ugliness of a beard; the prayer was granted, but her father crucified her all the same. Another name for her was St. Uncumber, a word which seems to derive from the fact that women prayed to her to be rid of their husbands.

Just as the theologians argued about whether Christ's divinity or humanity was predominant, so carvers were never sure whether to show the crucified Christ as ruler of the world or as suffering servant. Many Catalonian crucifixes show a half-naked Christ hanging from the cross. Barcelona again provides a good example: but even here the pain of the crucifixion is not stressed as it was in later cen-

128 Barcelona. F. Marés Museum. Crucifix

129 *above* Barcelona. F. Marés Museum. Crucifix
130 *right* Parma. Cathedral. Deposition
[102]

turies, and the crown is usually a regal one, not a crown of thorns. One remarkable crucifix at Barcelona even shows King David supporting Christ on the cross, and this must refer not only to Christ's ancestry but also to his kingship. In the following centuries, Germany led the way in presenting Christ on the cross with more realism and expressing more of his agony. But the chief Romanesque image of the Crucifixion is one of majesty and dignity.

Because the natural place to show the Crucifixion was on or above the altar, there is less stone carving of the scene in early medieval times. The separate figures also tend to be of wood and free-standing: the two usually shown are of course Mary and John, and they also are restrained in their grief during the Romanesque period. The idea of 'the sorrows of Mary' came later, together with renewed devotion

to her and mystical contemplation of Christ's own pain.

The other figures and symbols around the cross are perhaps best considered in the context of the following scene,
the Deposition[m]. A panel at Parma, by the great north
Italian sculptor, Antelami, presents a full and impressive
picture, which contains many of the elements that were used
in medieval iconography of the scene on Calvary. In the
central part of this panel we see Joseph of Arimathea standing on the right of Christ, and receiving his body as it is
brought down from the cross. Christ's hand is stretched out
towards his mother, who caresses it in her grief; here the
diagonal line of body and arm promotes a sense of movement in what would otherwise be a rather vertical group.
Between these two figures stands Ecclesia, the church, with
an angel tending her from above: she is receiving in a Com-

munion cup the blood which flows from Christ's side. In earlier pictures of the Crucifixion, this flow springs from the thrust of a spear or lance by a soldier[n]; to him, as to the centurion, the name Longinus, or spearman, was given in the apocryphal gospels. The full panel shows many more figures and symbols. All seem to have a certain stiffness and severity; but the carving is full of suppressed energy and rich in its devotional spirit. John and the mourning women are seen behind Mary on the right of Christ. On his left, Nicodemus stands on a ladder to free Christ's hand. Beyond him, matching Ecclesia, is the symbolic figure of the Synagogue, also attended by an angel but now having her old covenant displaced by the new. Behind her, the centurion and a second line of mourners approach, as though in a procession; below them, four soldiers animatedly settle what is to happen to Christ's robe. The two figures set in roundels at the top corners are the sun and moon. Their presence in representations of the Crucifixion has varied significance. They symbolize the presence of all creation, and not only the human part of it; and, just as the moon shines only with the light of the sun, so the Old Testament has meaning only in the light of the New. Sun and moon also stand for the two natures of Christ. In some representations they are shown veiling their faces: this is to indicate creation's horror at the scene, as displayed by an eclipse.

Antelami's carving of the Deposition, with its compact metallic figures, has links with Provence and also is almost Gothic in spirit. For a starker, more Romanesque, portrayal of the scene one may look to something earlier, the Externsteine carving. This image was cut from the rock, for a chapel built here in the early twelfth century, and it is understandably much damaged; but enough remains to show the carver's powerful sense of grief and distress at the scene. Here the dead Christ falls heavily on the contorted body of Joseph of Arimathea. Nicodemus above them wears the cap which regularly indicates a Jew of some standing. He has used not a ladder but something that looks like an ornate chair to reach the upper part of the cross: this support may in fact be a tree, or possibly the broken top of an antique column, symbol of the fall of the old religions. John here stands grieving in his more usual position, at the left side of Christ. The sun veils its face in eclipse. Beside it is the figure of God the Father, with two fingers of his right

131 *left* Externsteine. Deposition
132 S. Juan de las Abadesas. Monastery. Deposition

hand pointing downwards; the other hand cradles the soul of the dead Christ and holds the flag which symbolizes the Resurrection to come. This is a moving group, expressing the awe and reverence of Christianity in a place which had been numinous from earliest times but was often used for the worship of darker gods.

A third expressive Depositon can be seen in a set of wooden figures in the church of San Juan de las Abadesas. Here the two thieves appear (one of them, not seen in the illustration, a replacement following the Spanish Civil War); but they are only a kind of frame for the five superb figures in the centre. Mary and John are sensitive mourners; the difficulty of identifying John, who here, as often, looks very feminine, is lessened by the fact that he usually holds his gospel as a sign of who he is. Joseph and Nicodemus reach out tenderly to take the Lord down from the cross. The face of Christ is strangely powerful, yet compassionate: it is hard to think of any representation that is finer than this. On his forehead can be seen the front of a receptacle for the Host. Crucifixes were quite often used in early times to contain the reserved sacrament. It is for this reason that the group is sometimes known locally as 'The Mysteries'.

133 *right* Melle. St. Pierre church. Entombment
134 *opposite* Silos. Cloister. Entombment

Finally Christ is placed in the tomb. A beautiful capital at Melle shows a dignified dead Christ, with Joseph and Nicodemus bending reverently to their task as they lay the body down. An angel flies in above, a symbol of adoration: veneration of the dead Christ, whose sacrifice is his glory, was a feature of early Good Friday liturgies. More remote in style, and perhaps more Oriental in origin, is the impressive Entombment from the cloisters of Santo Domingo de Silos. Here the long thin figures of Joseph and Nicodemus and the dead Christ have the distinctive spiritual quality and refinement of vision which mark all the work at Silos. This brilliant plastic art, with its strange frozen effect, is not universally admired; but there are those who rank it with the Moissac sculpture as among the very finest Romanesque carving.

In other representations of the Entombment Mary and

John appear; their mourning comes to dominate the scene, and gradually to exclude Joseph and Nicodemus. But the separate scenes of the Lamentation and of the Virgin holding Christ on her lap (the Pietà) are later in date. The anointing of Christ's body is an early image, however: the spot in the Church of the Holy Sepulchre at Jerusalem where Christ was supposed to have been anointed is still pointed out, and the anointing stone itself was taken to Constantinople as a relic in the twelfth century. A fine capital at Dreux portrays the scene. The man at Christ's head who does the anointing wears the head-dress we have already seen on Nicodemus – the carvers' sign for a Jew: this is a reference to John's comment[o] that it was a Jewish practice to prepare a body for burial in this way.

Further anointing is prepared for the day after the Sabbath by the Marys and Salome[p]. Two representations of this are here shown. One is of stone, at Mozac, in the coarse but powerful style of the Auvergne; it is much easier to study than most capitals, since it now stands on the floor at the back of the church. The other carving of the scene is a small ivory panel from Cologne: the style is light and delicate, as befits the material. These show the very different ways in which two carvings can portray the women's loving care. By this time, however, anointing is no longer needed. The story is now not of Death but of Life.

135 *left* Dreux. Museum. Anointing
136 *above* Mozac. Abbey church. Women at the Tomb
137 *opposite* Cologne. Schnütgen Museum. Women at the Tomb

5. Resurrection and Judgment

'THE THIRD DAY he rose again from the dead', we say in the Apostles' Creed. But no human eye saw it happening, and for a long time carvers and painters shrank from portraying the Resurrection itself. Apart from one capital in Toulouse, which was perhaps influenced by an Ottonian miniature, there is no sculpture in Romanesque times of this key scene. Later, of course, it would become a popular subject: in the fourteenth and fifteenth centuries, many carved Nottingham alabasters and many church paintings would show a triumphant rising from the tomb, often with Christ stepping forth onto a sleeping soldier. By then, drama and liturgy had made it more natural to re-enact this moment; and the use of a soldier as a step confirms the thought that this portrayal is possible only because Passion plays have brought divine mysteries down to earth. Yet the carver in early medieval times keeps hidden, through reverence, the instant of Resurrection.

But there were other ways of expressing belief in the risen Christ. The preceding sentence of the Creed says, 'He descended into Hell'; and the reference is not simply to a Jewish Sheol, where the shades of the dead lie, but more to the great legend of Christ harrowing Hell, conquering the power of sin and death, and reclaiming the just souls who lived before his time. In the East, the emphasis was on the last of these: a famous fresco in the church of Saint Saviour in Chora at Istanbul shows Christ pulling up Adam with his right hand and Eve with his left. This whole theme – the Anastasis or Raising up – is a central one in Byzantine art. We have already seen that it appears also in Western carving: on the font at Eardisley, the rescuing of Adam is the essence of Christ's descent into Hell. But the West generally made more of the conquest of Satan, and of Christ's victory over death taking place in the unseen world before Easter Sunday. The elements of the story cannot be based, of course, on what the four evangelists tell us. But an apocryphal work, the Gospel of Nicodemus, tells of two sons of Simeon being restored to life in the convulsions of Good Friday: they describe how he who had shown power by the raising of Lazarus came down to Hell, carrying the cross of victory.

138 Tudela. Cathedral. Harrowing of Hell

There are echoes in this account of Psalm 24, of Isaiah 14, and of 1 Corinthians 15. It is therefore rich in its poetic echoes, even though the event described must be (like the Book of Revelation) right outside human experience. At Tudela one can just make out a further image, drawn from the book of Job, which became a familiar element in the world of the damned, both here and in scenes of the Last Judgment. 'Canst thou draw out Leviathan with a hook?' says God to Job[a]; and Leviathan, with gaping mouth, became a symbol of Hell, and Christ the symbol of one who could defeat even the Leviathan who stood for Hell. The cross of victory, and the just souls being saved, can also be seen in the Tudela carving; another feature often shown is a separate Satan being trodden underfoot. Here was Christ's victory over death, for others as well as for himself.

On a capital at St. Nectaire, the Harrowing of Hell is seen on one side, and on the other the women's visit to the empty tomb appears. This event, recorded in all four gospel

stories[b], was the commonest way of representing the Resurrection. The purpose of the visit is said by both Mark and Luke to have been the anointing of Christ's body. This purpose, already touched on at the end of the preceding chapter, was well-known through church drama: indeed the story was there filled out by scenes of the women buying spices in the market-place, before they encountered the angel (or angels) and heard the declaration that Christ was risen. Ways of showing the tomb itself varied in different ages. Sometimes it was a sarcophagus: a capital at St. Pons de Thomières, now in the Louvre, shows an angel demonstrating to the women that the tomb is empty – and Emile Mâle argues convincingly that here again medieval sacred drama has influenced the scene. But in other carvings the grander style of later tombs has affected the portrayal of the place where Christ was laid. Early building in Jerusalem had covered the traditional site of Christ's burial with something more ornate, and this is reflected in some of the earliest Christian art known to us. The capital at St. Nectaire has one side which shows the grander tradition, and in more contemporary terms. Beside the tomb are soldiers who no longer guard but sleep, and they wear medieval armour. Later Easter carvings would emphasize these well-armed soldiers, so that it is by seeing them, and the women, rather than by looking for any particular type of tomb, that this scene can be recognized.

Gradually it became possible to portray even the risen Christ as part of the scene in which the tomb is found empty. Sculptures at Monte Sant' Angelo, chaotic but wonderfully expressive, show a sequence of Passion events. On the left is an unusual Deposition. On the right, the angel greets the women below the tomb, while Peter and John hurry in from one side; on the other, towering above the scene and apparently invisible to his followers, a majestic Christ stands and points.

When the disciples are told the news, it is the youthful John who reaches the tomb first[c]. In a capital from Toulouse he stoops and looks in, leaning on a pillar, exhausted by his run, and amazed at what he sees. Peter will arrive later and, since he is always the man of action while John is the man of reverential love, he will be the first to venture right inside the tomb.

Meanwhile, the first recorded Resurrection appearance

139 *opposite, top* St. Pons. (now in the Louvre). Angel and empty Tomb

140 *opposite, below* St. Nectaire. Church. Sleeping soldiers

141 *above* Monte Sant' Angelo. Tomba dei Rotari. Passion scenes

142 *left* Toulouse. Musée des Augustins. John reaches the Tomb

143 *opposite* Hildesheim. Cathedral door. Christ & Mary Magdalene

of the risen Christ is to Mary Magdalene[d]: when he speaks her name, she recognizes at once that he is Jesus, not the gardener, and she falls at his feet. The scene on the doors at Hildesheim has a lyrical contrast in the curves of the two figures. Christ restrains Mary's wish to touch him, for he is already ascending to the Father, with the cross of victory in his hand; but the tenderness which accompanies the command 'Noli me tangere' is very evident. The tone of a capital at Autun is equally gentle: Mary is still holding in one hand the bowl of spices, with which she planned to anoint the dead Saviour, while Christ draws away from the other hand, which is outstretched towards his feet. Gislebertus, who was responsible for almost all the carvings at Autun, displays the very finest qualities of the Burgundian school of sculptors. His figures are long and mystical (whereas in Provence and Auvergne they tend to be broader and coarser); yet there is a natural and expressive air to them, and such distortion as the frame may demand is firmly controlled. The narrating of scenes that are both human and divine could hardly be better done. Less graceful, but still

powerful in its movement, is a capital at Saulieu, based on Gislebertus' carving of the scene: here the cloak of Christ, who dominates the picture, shows the folds and spirals that are characteristic of Romanesque art, deriving from the ornamentation of abstract carvings and manuscript illustrations.

Luke's first description of a Resurrection appearance comes in the moving story of the walk to Emmaus[e]. The two disciples learn only by stages, as they travel, why the death of Jesus in Jerusalem has a depth of meaning, and finally who their companion is. To see gradually the full meaning of Jesus' sacrifice, and so to see him as Christ, is the experience of many subsequent Christians, and not simply of Cleopas and the other disciple in Luke's story; and the recognition of Christ in the Breaking of Bread forms a fitting climax to the process. It was natural therefore that the two who walked to Emmaus should be seen by carvers as prototypes of those who later walked and followed: in particular they brought to mind the thought of pilgrimage.

The stranger who accompanies the two disciples to

144 *above* Autun. Cathedral. Christ and Mary Magdalene
145 *above, left* Saulieu. Abbey church. Christ and Mary Magdalene

146 *above* Silos. Cloister. Walk to Emmaus
147 *right* Silos. Cloister. Head of Christ

Emmaus was also in Romanesque times often portrayed as a pilgrim – indeed, the Latin word 'peregrinus' has both meanings. This feature may well have been first introduced in a Passion play and then taken up by the carvers. A fine relief in the cloister of Santo Domingo de Silos shows Christ with the cap and scrip of the pilgrims who passed that way on the road to Santiago de Compostela. His legs are crossed, to suggest motion, and his feet are bare – a special attribute

148 Autun. Cathedral. Halt at Emmaus

in medieval carving of God or Christ, of angels or disciples. There is wisdom and nobility in the head as he looks back at Cleopas and the other disciple. The stave on Christ's shoulder is clearly seen here too; and this, with the scrip, is an important clue in a recent piece of detective work.

At Autun there is a lively capital, which has long been admired and photographed. But its subject remained in doubt. The likeliest theory was that it represented the healing of the blind man at Jericho[f]. This was partly because of the small figure on the right: as he seems to be standing on top of a tree and opening a door, it was assumed that he was Zacchaeus, whose story[g] immediately follows that of the healing of the blind man. But a close study of the capital makes it plain that Christ is represented as a pilgrim, with scrip and stave. As George Zarnecki has shown, such representation is unique to the Emmaus scene; and thus he proves that what we see is in fact the moment at Emmaus when Christ made as if to go further but was urged by the two disciples to stay with them. The central figure can be seen to be a disciple, from the fact that he has a nimbus – though this is hard to detect in most reproductions; and the suggestion that he is pointing at his eye is due to a small stucco restoration in the capital by someone who misunderstood the scene. As for the small character on the right, he is the innkeeper at Emmaus opening a door; the belief that he was standing in a tree was due to a misunderstanding of one of the conventional features of Romanesque art. This capital shows a charming interplay between the main figures; and the interest of it is greater, now that its scene has been correctly interpreted as Emmaus rather than Jericho.

The cloister at Silos concerns itself, almost entirely, with events that follow the Crucifixion. The sculptor knows nothing of perspective or foreshortening: so, in the three reliefs where all the apostles appear, he places the figures in rows, one above the other. The Incredulity of Thomas[h] is perhaps the most successful of these scenes. The verticals of the other apostles contrast with the diagonals in the bottom left-hand corner, where Thomas reaches out to Christ's wounded side. The intensity of the spectators, with their severe, fixed gaze, makes a striking frame, even though their individuality is not so finely conceived as in another great carving on the road to Santiago, the tympanum at Moissac.

A more fluent rendering of Thomas' meeting with his risen Lord is to be seen on a superb capital at Nazareth. These capitals, the work of a French carver, were almost certainly hidden in the ground before they were ever put up and lay there for more than seven centuries. The sculptor has given his faces a distinctive soulful quality, and the drapery creates enchanting curves and circles. The resemblance in style, and in the surrounding architecture, to a capital at Plaimpied, near Bourges, has already been

149 *opposite* Silos. Cloister. Doubting Thomas
150 *below* Nazareth. Museum. Doubting Thomas

noticed. It cannot be claimed that this fine carving is anything other than metropolitan French work; but very few of the carvings now in France are more exciting in their vitality than the Nazareth capitals. Most of them represent legendary deeds of the apostles, and so do not properly belong here; but one more shall be admitted, to underline the expressive quality of this carver's remarkable work.

The Ascension[i] signifies the conclusion of Christ's visible work on earth. In portrayals of this event, the Virgin Mary is usually added to the company of the apostles, though the Bible says nothing of this. She has a place of honour in the centre, not only as Jesus' mother but also as a symbol of the church which he left behind. It is not easy to portray Christ convincingly in this scene. Sometimes, as at Silos, his head alone appears above a cloud. Sometimes, less happily, only his feet are seen, and everything above is shrouded in mist. Another tradition was to show him striding upwards to clasp the hand of God. But the representation which soon ousted all others was of a Christ being borne aloft by angels, often in an extended nimbus, or mandorla (the word is Italian for 'almond', denoting the shape). The stiffness of the central figure is often balanced, as at Collonges, by the animation of the watchers below, who are speaking of the event to each other as they witness Christ's glory. It is likely that the model for this Collonges tympanum was the portal at Cahors, which still has a fine lyrical quality, in spite of having been moved and restored. Here the tympanum is filled out by angels plunging downwards from above, by panels of the martyrdom of Stephen, the cathedral's patron

saint, and by the Virgin and line of apostles standing below. But the centre is best seen in detail, without these additions. Christ in the mandorla is a noble figure. On either side angels bend outward in contrasting curves, as they often do in this scene. Sometimes this implies effort, but here they are plainly speaking to the apostles below.

Their words to the apostles are surely those of the two men in white robes who say, 'This same Jesus, which is taken up from you into heaven, shall so come again in like manner as ye have seen him go into heaven'. For this reason, Christ's appearance in Glory is often represented in a way very similar to his Ascension: he leaves the world and reigns above in the same majestic pose, suggestive more of heaven than of earth. The scene of Christ in Glory, or the 'Majestas Domini', was a favourite subject for a tympanum in medieval times. Such portrayal of the Lord in triumph had long been a special theme for the painted apse of a church; the tympanum mirrored the apse's shape, as well as having links with the pagan arch of triumph. This depiction of Christ in Glory drew on much Old Testament imagery, from Isaiah, Ezekiel, and Daniel, but also related most closely to Christ, the Saviour of the World, through the fourth chapter of Revelation. Of the representations which can be seen in England, the best known is over the Prior's

151 *opposite, left* Nazareth. Museum. Apostles
152 *above* Silos. Cloister. Ascension
153 *opposite, below* Collonges. Church. Ascension
154 *above, left* Cahors. Cathedral. Ascension

155 *above* Ely. Cathedral. Christ in Glory
156 *opposite, right* Barnack. Church. Christ in Glory
157 *below* Barfreston. Church. Christ in Glory
158 *opposite, left* Lugo. Cathedral. Christ in Glory

Door at Ely cathedral. The curves of the supporting angels here follow that of the mandorla. Christ is seated, whereas usually in western representations of the Ascension proper he is standing; his right hand is raised in blessing, while cross and scroll are to his left. Not far away, at Barnack, is one of the noblest English sculptures of Christ in his Glory, as God. Again the right hand gives a blessing, and the other hand closes over a book which rests on his left knee. But this is a fragment only. A much fuller picture of Christ in Glory can be seen at Barfreston, in Kent; this imposing tympanum is one of the few outstanding Romanesque works in the south-east corner of England. These three English versions of the 'Majestas Domini' may well have used French and Spanish equivalents as their models. But there is a difference in style, for all these three have a rather flat and linear quality; this may be due to the persistence of Anglo-Saxon and Viking influences in England well after the Norman conquest.

A theme which is as important as that of Christ in Glory could easily be illustrated from many churches throughout Western Europe. Two will suffice to point the contrast between English and Continental work; both are from the final stages of the Pilgrim Route to Santiago. At Lugo, where the head is a better restoration than one sometimes

159 Carrión de los Condes. St James church. Christ in Glory

sees, there is a tall dignity in the seated figure; the projection of the knees (often a problem) is skilfully tackled. At Carrión de los Condes the left hand again grasps the book on the left knee. But the significant feature here is the appearance of the four creatures around Christ. These can be seen in many of the finest carvings of Christ in his Glory. They are sometimes spoken of as the tetramorphs – the four shapes. Their origin lies in a vision of Ezekiel's[j] which refers in a rather mysterious way to man, lion, ox, and eagle. This vision is taken up in Revelation[k], where the same four creatures sing praises round the throne of God. They are normally shown in the carver's regular order of priority, in which high is greater than low, and the right of the throne greater than the left. So man is dominant, as the lord of all creation; lower in standing are the lion, lord of wild animals, the eagle, lord of birds, and the ox, lord of domesticated animals. But more symbolical meanings were soon added. One took the creatures as representing four stages of Christ's life: he was a man in his birth, a calf in his sacrificial death, a lion in his resurrection (see page 33), and an eagle in his ascent to heaven. A much commoner interpretation made the creatures stand for the four evangelists – the man being Matthew, the lion Mark, the ox Luke, and the eagle John. It required some ingenuity to explain these four attributions. The usual solution was to say that they referred to the beginnings of the gospels: Matthew starts with a human genealogy, Mark with a voice crying in the wilderness, Luke with the sacrifice of Zechariah, and John with a meditation

160 Vézelay. Abbey church.
   Pentecost

on the Word which takes the believer up to heaven. These symbols of the evangelists persisted; the lion of St. Mark is particularly well known, because of Venice. Later sculpture, however, often forgot the four creatures and showed the evangelists as men writing instead.

One of the finest of all tympana portrays the day of Pentecost[l]. It is set in the inner narthex of the great basilica of St. Mary Magdalene at Vézelay. Several alternative explanations of this powerful sculpture have been proposed. The strongest of these is that, since neither the Holy Spirit nor the Virgin Mary is shown, the carving must portray Christ's command to the apostles to go and make disciples of all nations[m]. This, as we shall see, is certainly an element in the composition. But it seems to me more likely that the central theme is the day of Pentecost: there are other portrayals in the twelfth century of Christ sending rays of light forth from his hands, rather than of a symbolic dove, when artists wish to denote the outpouring of the Spirit on the first Whitsunday. In the centre of the tympanum here is a grave elongated Christ in a mandorla. The wind stirs his robe, which is decorated with the characteristic whirls and eddies, and he sits sideways; this disposes of a particular problem – that a seated figure facing forward on a flat tympanum can easily become so three-dimensional that it makes the whole composition awkward. The apostles are all movement and inspiration around the central Christ. A semi-circle of compartments surrounds the main tympanum: in these the apostles, each of whom was believed to have preached the gospel to a different part of the world, heal and evangelize. Their message is received with joy and animation, even by the cynocephali (that is, men with the heads of dogs). Strange creatures, taken from the writings of antiquity, are still more in evidence along the lintel: there, on the left, peoples of the earth are moving inwards to St. Peter and St. Paul (representing the church), and on the right those who are still pagan appear. Scythians with huge ears and pygmies needing a ladder to climb on horseback can be seen. The theme is therefore the baptizing of the whole world with the Holy Spirit, even as John the Baptist (who is visible on the central trumeau) baptized with water. It was a theme that might have had an extra relevance here in the early twelfth century, in view of the close connection of Cluny and Vézelay with the crusades.

The apostles setting forth to convert the world can also be seen in several fine tympana at Angoulême, of which one is shown here. The whole west front of this cathedral is decorated with beautiful individual items. If they do not seem to cohere, that is partly because of the extensive nineteenth-century reconstruction of this façade; but it is also partly because here, more than anywhere, the Ascension and all that follows it are combined in a single theme. At the top Christ rises to heaven, with the tetramorphs around him (but with unusual placing). His commission to the apostles is plain; but so is the fact of his return to judge the world.

Of all themes at the western end of a cathedral, the Last Judgment is perhaps the most potent. The west was the region of darkness and doom: its portal was the sign which warned everyone entering for worship that every action had eternal consequences. It is not surprising therefore that

162 Angoulême. Cathedral. Ascension and Glory

many of the very finest sculptors of the Romanesque period concerned themselves with the Last Judgment; their message may seem to us to be a grim one, but to those who toiled in dark days to obey the commands of Christ it could well have been a message of hope, and not solely a warning. The world was moving towards a final fulfilment of God's purposes: in the kingdom to come the last would be first, provided only that they had been faithful, and those who seemed to pluck the pleasures of this world would be last. When the trumpet sounded[n], the dead would leave their tombs, as at Tudela; in early times all would be shown as being of the same age – in their early thirties – since the age of Christ at his death was held to be the age at which all the dead would later rise. Then everyone would appear before the Judgment Seat: in the sonorous words of the 'Dies Irae',

> Tuba mirum spargens sonum
> Per sepulchra regionum
> Coget omnes ante thronum.

Yet the earliest Romanesque sculptures of the Last Judg-

161 *top* Angoulême. Cathedral. Apostles set forth
163 *above* Tudela. Cathedral. Resurrection of the dead

[127]

ment do not concern themselves with the saved and the damned, but with the worship and praise of Christ the Lord. An eighth-century commentary on the Apocalypse, by Beatus of Spain, had a profound influence, through manuscripts, on the image men had of the Last Things; and representations of the end of the world naturally focused on the description in Revelation of the heavenly worship which John the Divine saw in his vision°. On the tympanum at Moissac, Christ the King is the still centre of a turbulence of praise and adoration. Wearing the polygonal crown of the old emperors, he gazes down with the splendour of a sovereign and the severity of a judge. Flanking him are the four creatures, here holding books as a clear sign that they represent the four evangelists; beyond them two sublime seraphs curve inwards in ecstatic worship. The rest of the tympanum is filled by the four and twenty elders, looking eagerly inward and upward to Christ. There is perhaps nothing in Romanesque art that is so impressive as these strong and dignified faces: all are different, yet all are

earnest and adoring with their solemn gaze. Each, in Revelation, holds a harp and golden bowls of incense, which are the prayers of the saints; in carvings these are often represented by a viol and a vial (or chalice).

In some representations the elders are ranged round an arch; this, as we have noticed earlier, is a suitable setting for a number of people, though not for a narrative scene. We see them so placed in Oloron Ste. Marie, as in many places along the pilgrim route – including Santiago itself. The instruments are sometimes more diverse than at Moissac; but always there is the gravity and poise of kings in a heavenly vision paying honour to the King of Kings.

This early south-western picture of the Last Things does not endure. In the Last Judgment at Beaulieu, though it is much influenced by the Moissac tympanum, the heavenly worship of the Apocalypse no longer has pride of place. Here, Christ spreads his arms wide, in the attitude which he had on the cross; he wears no crown, for he now returns as he was on earth, the Redeemer who pleads his own sacrifice

164 *opposite, top* Moissac. Abbey church. Last Judgment
165 *opposite, below* Moissac. Abbey church. Elders
166 *below* Oloron Ste. Marie. Ste. Marie church. Elders
167 *above* Beaulieu. Abbey church. Last Judgment

rather than the King who sits above mortal dangers. The splendid central figure is all. Behind him is 'the sign of the Son of Man'[p], a cross, and on each side angels blow trumpets to awaken the dead. All around him the apostles take part in the judgment, as they were promised that they should[q]. Beneath him the dead rise from their tombs; and on the lintels there are symbols of Hell, though we see little of the damned or of the act of judging itself.

This pattern, of Christ coming on the Last Day as the Saviour who knows what it is to be a man, with everlasting rewards and punishments for human sins, became the pattern also in Northern France. In Burgundy and Auvergne too the picture was one of Christ returning to earth, sometimes displaying his wounds and the Instruments of his Passion, to judge mankind as a man divides the sheep from the goats[r]. The image of the Last Day was no longer based on the vision from Revelation but on one of Christ's most direct parables: it warned even the most unlearned of people that a judgment, which might happen the very next day, would be based on their ordinary actions.

The tympanum at Conques is essentially one for the com-

mon people. Though Languedoc is near, there is little of the noble, other-worldly quality that marks the sculpture of Toulouse and Moissac; the influence is rather that of the Auvergne, with its stubby, naturalistic figures and its added messages. The representations of the saved and the damned are easy enough to follow; but here they do not have, to my mind, the mysterious appeal of an event that lies outside human experience. Some find this tympanum impressive, because of its general structure and narrative style (and perhaps also because of the peace and beauty of its setting); but the figures have a faint suggestion of the comic strip for modern eyes, whereas Moissac and Autun have a total solemnity. What is very imposing, however, is the dominant Christ at the centre. His expression is both compassionate and decisive, as he raises his right hand for the saved and lowers his left hand for the damned.

Very different are the outspread hands of Christ in the magnificent Last Judgment portal at Autun. Indeed the whole tympanum offers a striking contrast to that at Conques. Not only are the figures elongated, as in a vision: they also seem to seize the viewer in a way that the more

168 *opposite, above* Conques. Abbey church. Last Judgment
169 *opposite, below* Conques. Abbey church. Christ the Judge
170 *above* Autun. Cathedral. Last Judgment

ordinary figures of Conques never do despite the horror they portray. That perhaps is why the Autun tympanum was thought to be too crude and terrible and was covered in plaster from 1766 till 1837; the result is that it is now very well preserved. On the left of Christ, St. Michael is weighing souls (an image originally derived from Egypt); a cheating devil here, as often, tries to tip the balance, like some dishonest grocer. Yet for many the weighing seems hardly needed, since the dead, even as they rise to life, appear to be already aware of their fate; and one of the supreme horrors, among the torments of the damned, is the grim pair of hands below the scales that is seizing one sinner at the moment when he leaves the grave. On the right of Christ there are some charming vignettes of the souls who are saved: looking at the tympanum in detail, one can see, for example, the tender ministrations of St. Peter, and, in the line below, the three children clinging to an angel, the husband and wife, and the pair of pilgrims. For all the tensions of this Hell, the real triumph of Gislebertus is to have made so sublime a picture of the joys of Heaven. For Paradise is not easy to convey for a carver, who cannot make use of the light and the music which were Dante's answer. The saved pose for him the real challenge: all too often they look dull and self-satisfied, while all drama and deep feeling are left to the lost souls. Indeed, it has been cynically said that one of the chief delights of the medieval heaven was the admirable view it afforded

171 *opposite, below* Ferrara. Cathedral. The Damned
172 *above* Malmesbury. Abbey church. Apostles
173 *opposite, above* Malmesbury. Abbey church. Apostles.

of the torments of the damned. Some later carvers engaged keenly, and even sadistically, in depicting such torments. The façade at Ferrara is a relatively mild example.

To carve visions beyond this world is perhaps the severest test of narrative sculpture. Yet the purpose of imagining the unimaginable was to create the right impression, of awe and worship, in the mind of the beholder. Beauty, says Lessing in his 'Laocoon', is best conveyed not by itemizing the finer points of the beloved or the features of the landscape, but by showing the impression it makes on those who look at it; the same may be true of holiness. The way in which the carvers represent the elders of Moissac, or the bystanders at Angoulême, tells us vividly something of the nature of the divine vision and how we ourselves may react to it. For a final picture of men seeing something more than human, let us turn to Malmesbury Abbey. Each side of the porch here shows us the reaction of the apostles to the scene in the tympanum of Christ in Majesty, or Christ at his Ascension. The depiction of these apostles is most sensitive, with the same elongated style that we have seen at Autun and in Western France. St. Peter on one side, and St. Paul on the other, look towards Christ. So do the angels and the two single figures bowing their heads beneath them. The other eight apostles talk to each other in pairs. The message for the faithful might well be that they should both see Christ's glory and reflect with others on what they see.

The central purpose of religious sculpture must be to kindle feelings and evoke a response in those who look at it. Adam and Eve, proclaiming human sinfulness, point the Christian forward to the wonderful grace by which God in Christ has redeemed sin. Old Testament characters are revered because in them, as in a glass darkly, is seen the greater truth of the gospel and the church which will appear later. The Nativity story moves the believer because of the humility of a Saviour who came down as a helpless child. The events of Jesus' Ministry, by contrast, win the heart by their use of power and authority wholly in the service of love. The Passion story rouses the strongest feelings of all – so strong indeed that both artist and worshipper must beware of settling for sentimentality and excess; it is significant that the word 'maudlin' derives from the mawkish lack of restraint with which art in later ages portrayed Mary Magdalene. Finally, Resurrection and Judgment would be only remote tales if they did not make a vivid appeal to the strongest of man's hopes and fears.

Romanesque carving has great power to arouse devotion by stirring the feelings of the believer. Its deepest reality lies not in appearances but in emotions – yet emotions under control; it does not embarrass by being crude or over-sentimental, as many later works of religious art do. Rather, it has a gravity and poignancy which have led many twentieth-century sculptors, like Barlach, to return to this idiom as something eternal in its simplicity.

The straightforward feelings of medieval men and women towards their Creator and Saviour might seem, for people today, too literal and naïve. Yet the realistic and rational responses of our day sometimes appear too cold, and the emotional responses sometimes too insubstantial. Our need today is perhaps to recapture direct and firmly-based feelings that are neither coldly rational nor sentimentally emotional. One possible way of doing this is to learn from the spontaneous worship of non-Western countries, cutting through the web of twentieth-century sophistication and simplifying devotion and awe. Another way is, through carvings, to cast oneself into the powerful and direct worship of medieval man. To make this possible, indeed exciting, has been one of the purposes of this book.

The Villein's Bible

References

Chapter 1

[a] Genesis 2.4-3.24
[b] Philippians 2.6
[c] 1 Peter 3.19
[d] Genesis 4.1-16
[e] Genesis 4.17-24
[f] Genesis 6.8-9.29
[g] Genesis 22.1-14
[h] Matthew 12.42
   Luke 11.31
[i] 1 Kings 3.16-28
[j] Matthew 12.40
   Luke 11.29-32
[k] 1 Samuel 17.1-54
[l] Daniel 6.16-23
[m] Judges 14.6
[n] Judges 16.23-31
[o] Judges 15.15-17
[p] Numbers 22.21-30
[q] Numbers 24.17
[r] 2 Kings 2.11
[s] Exodus 14.5-31
[t] John 3.14
[u] Exodus 34.29-35

Chapter 2

[a] Matthew 1.18-2.23
[b] Luke 1.26-2.40
[c] Isaiah 7.14
[d] Isaiah 1.3
[e] Habakkuk 3.2
[f] Psalm 91.13
[g] Leviticus 12.1-8

Chapter 3

[a] Matthew 3.13-17
   Mark 1.1-11
   Luke 3.21-22
[b] John 3.30
[c] Genesis 1.2
[d] Luke 3.22
[e] Psalm 2.7
[f] 1 Kings 7.23-26
[g] Matthew 14.3-12
   Mark 6.17-29
[h] Matthew 4.1-11
   Luke 4.1-13
[i] John 2.1-11
[j] Matthew 4.18-22
   Mark 1.16-20
   Luke 5.1-11
[k] John 4.1-30
[l] Matthew 26.6-13
[m] Mark 14.3-9
[n] Luke 7.36-50
[o] John 12.1-8
[p] Matthew 17.1-9
   Mark 9.2-10
   Luke 9.28-36
[q] Luke 16.19-31
[r] Matthew 25.1-13
[s] Mark 5.25-34
   Luke 8.43-48
[t] John 11.1-44

Chapter 4

[a] Matthew 21.1-11
   Mark 11.1-10
   Luke 19.29-38
   John 12.12-18
[b] Psalm 118.25-27

[c] Zechariah 9.9
[d] Matthew 26.14-16
   Mark 14.10-11
   Luke 22.3-6
[e] Matthew 26.20-29
   Mark 14.17-25
   Luke 22.14-46
   John 13.1-38
   1 Corinthians 11.23-26
[f] Matthew 14.13-21
       15.32-39
   Mark 6.32-44
       8.1-10
   Luke 9.11-17
   John 6.1-14
[g] Matthew 26.36-46
   Mark 14.32-42
   Luke 22.40-46
[h] Matthew 26.47-56
   Mark 14.43-50
   Luke 22.47-53
   John 18.1-12
[i] Matthew 26.69-75
   Mark 14.66-72
   Luke 22.54-62
   John 18.15-27
[j] Matthew 27.11-26
   Mark 15.2-15
   Luke 23.1-25
   John 18.29-19.16
[k] Matthew 27.33-56
   Mark 15.16-41
   Luke 23.32-49
   John 19.17-37
[l] John 19.37
   Revelation 1.7 and 1.13
[m] Matthew 27.57-61
   Mark 15.42-47
   Luke 23.50-56
   John 19.38-42

[n] John 19.34
[o] John 19.40
[p] Mark 16.1-2
   Luke 24.1

Chapter 5

[a] Job 41.1-34
[b] Matthew 28.1-10
   Mark 26.1-8
   Luke 24.1-12
   John 20.1-13
[c] John 20.3-10
[d] John 20.11-18
[e] Luke 24.13-35
[f] Luke 18.35-43
[g] Luke 19.1-10
[h] John 20.24-29
[i] Luke 24.50-51
   Acts. 1.1-11
[j] Ezekiel 1.10
[k] Revelation 4.7
[l] Acts 2.1-47
[m] Matthew 28.18-20
[n] 1 Corinthians 15.52
[o] Revelation 4.1-5.14
[p] Matthew 24.30
[q] Matthew 19.28
[r] Matthew 25.31-46

F R A N C E

Dreux
Paris
Pompierre

Seine

Loire
Vézelay
St. Aignan
Charité-sur-Loire
Dijon
Saulieu
Autun
Plaimpied
Vouvant
Chauvigny
Gargilesse
Cluny
Anzy-le-Duc
Melle
Neuilly-en-Donjon
Charlieu
Aulnay
Mozac
Angoulême
Clermont-Ferrand
St. Nectaire
Issoire
Lubersac
Collonges
Beaulieu
Souillac
Conques
Cahors
Moissac
Avignon
Arles
Toulouse
St. Gilles du Gard
St Pons de Thomières
Oloron
Ste Marie

0   100 Mls
0   150 Km

Verona

Castell'Arquato

Fidenza

Parma

Modena

Po

Venice

Ferrara

Lucca

Pisa

Arno

Arezzo

I T A L Y

Monte S. Angelo

Benevento

Bari

Santa Maria
a Cerrate

Monreale

S I C I L Y

0   100 Mls

0   150 Km

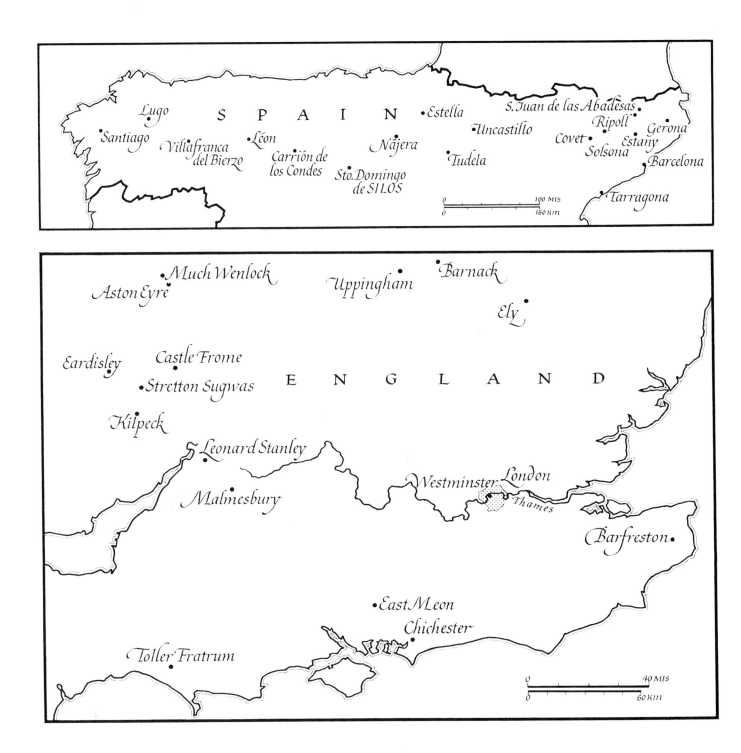

SPAIN

Lugo
Santiago
Villafranca del Bierzo
Léon
Carrión de los Condes
Sto. Domingo de SILOS
Nájera
Estella
Uncastillo
Tudela
S. Juan de las Abadesas
Ripoll
Covet
Solsona
Estany
Gerona
Barcelona
Tarragona

0   100 MIS
0   160 Km

ENGLAND

Much Wenlock
Aston Eyre
Uppingham
Barnack
Ely
Eardisley
Castle Frome
Stretton Sugwas
Kilpeck
Leonard Stanley
Malmesbury
Westminster London
Thames
Barfreston
East Meon
Chichester
Toller Fratrum

0   40 MIS
0   60 Km

List of Illustrations

(those with Roman numerals are colour plates appearing between pages 72 and 73)

1 Old Testament

1	Modena	Cathedral	Creation of Adam and Eve
2	Modena	Cathedral	The Fall
3	East Meon	Church	Creation of Adam and Eve
4	East Meon	Church	Adam, Eve and the serpent
5	Santiago	Cathedral	God and Adam
6	Autun	Museum	Eve
7	Hildesheim	Cathedral door	God, Adam, and Eve
8	Cluny	Museum	God, Adam, and Eve
9	Uncastillo	Santa Maria church	God, Adam, and Eve
10	Hildesheim	Cathedral door	Eve suckling Cain
11	Pisa	Cathedral door	Magi, with Fall of Man
12	Barcelona	F. Marés Museum	Crucifix, with Adam
13	Eardisley	Church font	Christ saves Adam
14	St. Gilles du Gard	Abbey church	Cain and Abel make their offerings
15	Monreale	Cathedral door	Cain kills Abel
16	Hildesheim	Cathedral door	Cain kills Abel
17	Autun	Cathedral	God questions Cain
18	Modena	Cathedral	Lamech kills Cain
19	Autun	Cathedral	Lamech kills Cain
20	Monreale	Cathedral door	Noah
21	Akhtamar	Church	Abraham and Isaac
22	Barcelona	Museum of Catalan art	Abraham and Isaac
23	Najera	Abbey church	Judgment of Solomon
24	Westminster	Abbey	Judgment of Solomon
25	Akhtamar	Church	David and Goliath
26	St. Aignan	Church	Daniel and the lions
27	Worms	Cathedral	Daniel and the lions
28	Stretton Sugwas	Church	Samson and the lion
29	Moissac	Abbey cloister	Samson and the lion
30	Avignon	(now in Fogg Museum, Cambridge, Mass.)	Samson pulls down the temple
31	Akhtamar	Church	Samson
32	Saulieu	Abbey church	Balaam
33	Fidenza	Cathedral	Elijah
34	Novgorod	Cathedral door	Elijah
35	Hildesheim	Cathedral font	Moses crosses the Red Sea
36	Augsburg	Cathedral door	Moses and the serpent
37	Moissac	Abbey church	Prophet (perhaps Jeremiah)
38	Souillac	Abbey church	Isaiah
39	Santiago	Cathedral	David

2 Nativity

40	Moissac	Abbey church	Annunciation
41	Conques	Abbey church	Annunciation
42	Monreale	Cathedral cloister	Annunciation
I	Gerona	Cathedral cloister	Annunciation
43	Villafranca del Bierzo	St. James church	Annunciation
44	Santiago	Cathedral	Annunciation
45	Castell' Arquato	Church	Isaiah prophesies Christ's birth
II	Barcelona	Cathedral	Visitation
46	Silos	Cloister	Visitation
47	Gargilesse	Church	Nativity
48	Santa Maria a Cerrate	Church	Nativity
49	Estany	Cloister	Nativity
50	Pisa	Cathedral door	Nativity
51	Ferrara	Cathedral	Nativity scenes
III	Cologne	Sankt Maria im Kapitol, church door	The shepherds
IV	Chauvigny	Church of St. Peter	The shepherds
52	Santiago	San Benito church	Three kings worship
53	Najera	Abbey church	Three kings worship
54	Autun	Cathedral	Three kings worship
55	Autun	Cathedral	Joseph
56	Neuilly-en-Donjon	Church	Three kings worship
57	Toulouse	Musée des Augustins	Three kings worship
58	Anzy-le-Duc	(now in museum of Paray-le Monial)	Virgin and Child
59	Covet	Church	Virgin and Child
60	Najera	Abbey church	Virgin and Child
61	Solsona	Cathedral	Virgin and Child
62	Léon	Cathedral museum	Virgin and Child, with monk
63	Venice	Cathedral	Virgin
64	Pisa	Cathedral door	Presentation
65	Hildesheim	Cathedral door	Presentation
66	Novgorod	Cathedral door	Presentation
67	Tarragona	Cathedral cloister	Three kings sleep
68	Autun	Cathedral	Three kings sleep
69	Estella	San Pedro church	Herod orders massacre
70	Pisa	Cathedral door	Massacre of the Innocents
71	Estany	Cloister	Flight into Egypt
72	Autun	Cathedral	Flight into Egypt
73	Saulieu	Abbey church	Flight into Egypt
74	Pisa	Cathedral door	Flight into Egypt

3 Ministry

4 Passion

110	Pisa	Cathedral door	Christ's entry into Jerusalem
111	Pompierre	Church	Christ's entry into Jerusalem
112	Aston Eyre	Church	Christ's entry into Jerusalem
113	Modena	Cathedral	Judas and Caiaphas
114	Verona	S. Zeno church door	Last Supper
115	Issoire	Church	Last Supper
116	Lugo	Cathedral	Last Supper
117	Dijon	Museum	Last Supper
118	Vouvant	Church	Last Supper
119	Autun	Cathedral	Christ washes the disciples' feet
120	Estany	Cloister	Christ washes the disciples' feet
121	Benevento	Cathedral door	Agony in the Garden
122	St. Gilles du Gard	Abbey church	Arrest of Christ
123	St. Gilles du Gard	Abbey church	Peter and Malchus
124	Verona	S. Zeno church door	Arrest of Christ
125	Benevento	Cathedral door	Arrest of Christ
126	Modena	Cathedral	Peter's denial
127	Hildesheim	Cathedral door	Christ before Pilate
V	Lucca	Cathedral	Volto Santo
VI	Barcelona	Museum of Catalan Art	Majestad
VII	Cologne	Diocesan Museum	Crucifix
128	Barcelona	F. Marés Museum	Crucifix
129	Barcelona	F. Marés Museum	Crucifix
130	Parma	Cathedral	Deposition
131	Externsteine		Deposition
132	S. Juan de las Abadesas	Monastery	Deposition
VIII	S. Juan de las Abadesas	Monastery	Head of Christ
133	Melle	St. Pierre church	Entombment
134	Silos	Cloister	Entombment
135	Dreux	Museum	Anointing
136	Mozac	Abbey church	Women at the Tomb
137	Cologne	Schnütgen Museum	Women at the Tomb

5 Resurrection and Judgment

Acknowledgments

I should never have had the interest and enjoyment of putting this book together if I had not been very fortunate in four particular respects:

Serenissima Travel invited me to lead groups for them on visits abroad, often following itineraries that I was allowed to devise, and to talk in a general way about the styles and periods of what we saw.

The staff of the Public Library at Gerrards Cross were active and friendly in seeking even the most obscure books for which I put in a card and, having secured them, were patient about their return.

My son, Tim, acquired a word-processor which, during some school holidays, he cheerfully lent to me and backed with advice and material.

My wife, Fiona, with a generosity that is her natural idiom, enthusiastically read what I wrote, even though Romanesque art might not be her first choice for illustrating the Bible she knows and loves.

To these I owe a special debt. But there were others who gave great help in translating an idea into a book:

Euan Cameron, of Barrie and Jenkins, Dr William Horbury, dean of Corpus Christi College, Cambridge, and Professor George Zarnecki, doyen of Romanesque scholars, read the first draft of my text and offered most useful comments.

The Courtauld Institute kindly gave to a very mature student the run of their library and Conway collection.

Mary Jane Gibson and Peter Guy, the picture researcher and designer chosen by Barrie and Jenkins, skilfully sought out and deployed the illustrations that I wanted, without which the book would be nothing.

Robert Runcie, despite the cares which he carries so lightly and wisely as Archbishop of Canterbury, offered to commend the book to many who might otherwise ignore it.

So I have many causes for gratitude. But nobody except myself is to blame if you find that your favourite carving has been omitted or your favourite opinion slighted.

Select Bibliography

Anderson, M.D. *The Imagery of British Churches* 1955
Atroshenko, V.I. and Collins, J. *Origins of the Romanesque* 1985
Aubert, M. *L'art Roman en France* 1961
Beckwith, J. *Early Medieval Art* 1964
Boase, T.S.R. *English Art 1100-1216* 1953
Crichton, G.H. *Romanesque Sculpture in Italy* 1954
Decker, H. *Romanesque Art in Italy* 1958
Deschamps, P. *French Sculpture of the Romanesque period* 1930
Domke, H. et al. *Romanesque Europe* 1958
Focillon, H. *The Art of the West – Romanesque Art* 1963
Grivot, D. and Zarnecki, G. *Gislebertus, Sculptor of Autun* 1961
Hearn, M.F. *Romanesque Sculpture* 1981
Keyser, C.E. *A List of Norman Tympana and Lintels* 1927
Lasko, P. *Ars Sacra 800-1200* 1972
Mâle, E. *Religious Art in France: The Twelfth Century* 1978
Oursel, R. *Floraison de la Sculpture Romane* 1976
  (and other books in the Zodiaque series)
Pevsner, N. *et al. The Buildings of England* 1951 onwards
Porter, A.K. *Romanesque Sculpture of the Pilgrimage Roads* 1966
Schiller, G. *Iconography of Christian Art* 1971-72
Souchal, F. *Art of the Early Middle Ages* 1968
Stone, L. *Sculpture in Britain, the Middle Ages* 1955
various *English Romanesque Art 1066-1200* (Arts Council Catalogue) 1984
various *Larousse Encyclopaedia of Byzantine and Medieval Art* 1963
Zarnecki, G. *English Romanesque Sculpture 1066-1140* 1951
Zarnecki, G. *Later English Romanesque Sculpture 1140-1210* 1953
Zarnecki, G. 'Romanesque' in the Herbert *History of Art and Architecture* 1989

Photocredits

Index